LOW-SUGAR COOKING

Healthy, delicious recipes using only the sweetness
that Nature intended.

Cover illustrations:

Front: Exotic Fruit Salad (page 143).
Back: Chocolate Pots (page 137).

In the same series
COOKING FOR DIABETES
FAST FOOD — REAL FOOD
LOW-FAT COOKERY
NO-SALT COOKERY

A Here'sHealth Guide to

LOW-SUGAR
C·O·O·K·I·N·G

Delicious dishes for a reduced-sugar diet

by

JACQUI HINE

THORSONS PUBLISHING GROUP
Wellingborough, Northamptonshire

Rochester, Vermont

First published 1987

© JACQUI HINE 1987

2 4 6 8 10 9 7 5 3 1

British Library Cataloguing in Publication Data

Hine, Jacqui
Here's health low-sugar cooking:
appetizing recipes that are low in sugar
but high in flavour and health.
1. Sugar-free diet — Recipes
I. Title
641.5'638   RM237.85

ISBN 0-7225-1371-2

Printed in Great Britain by
Hazell Watson & Viney Limited,
Member of the BPCC Group,
Aylesbury, Bucks

CONTENTS

FOREWORD

Tooth decay and gum disease could become dental diseases of the past if only we take the decision to cut back on the amount of sugar that we eat in our diet. Not only would we look and feel better without bad teeth, but also it would save us from the discomfort, inconvenience and expense of lengthy and complicated dental treatment. This does not mean that we should give up going to the dentist; rather it means that we should visit our dentist regularly and work with him to look after our teeth for life.

But the most important health measure for preventing tooth decay is sugar control. It begins with avoiding adding sugar to baby foods or giving a sugary drink in a feeding bottle. We also know that the quantity of sugar eaten at one time affects the quantity of plaque produced as well as our general health. However, if sugar is eaten frequently in cups of tea or coffee, snacks between meals, and sweets, this will affect the total time during which tooth decay is going on.

Good oral health is within our grasp if we brush our teeth thoroughly and eat less sugar, less often.

'Low-Sugar Cooking' promotes the sweetness of natural foods to help reduce the quantity of added refined sugar to the diet. The following pages are packed with helpful suggestions and recipes to show just how simple this can be — an excellent way to healthier teeth through a healthier diet.

Margaret Seward MDS, FDS, RCS
Editor, British Dental Journal
London

INTRODUCTION

This book is about sugar — not how to make use of it, but how to use LESS of it! Most people are born with a tendency to like sweetness and we tend to develop this by eating food saturated with sugar. Recent medical reports suggest that too much sugar in our diet not only causes tooth decay, but obesity and other related diseases. Even more recent reports suggest that other forms of cooked carbohydrates when eaten with other foods could also be responsible for tooth decay, and research continues in this field.[1] No-one, however, is in any doubt that large quantities of refined sugar taken at frequent intervals throughout the day are unhealthy, but that if sugars and starches are used in a sensible way, they can form a valuable part of our diet.

Most foods contain natural sugar, which, if eaten in its natural state, provide us with a valuable source of energy. By their very structure we are prevented from over-eating. The problems occur when the sugar is isolated and concentrated into 100 per cent pure refined sugar. It's very easy to over-eat in this form and our bodies were not designed to cope with such high influxes of sugar.

Even if you don't take sugar in your tea and coffee, and never eat sweets, you may still be eating several ounces (grammes) of sugar every day because the food industry add sugar to nearly every product, both sweet and savoury.

No-one is suggesting that we eliminate sugar completely from the diet, indeed, this would be both unnecessary and impractical, but the advice from medical sources is that we should reduce our sugar consumption by half and meet our energy requirements with other, more nutritious foods. This means re-educating our over-developed palates to accept and enjoy less sweet food. For the young, it means not being introduced to highly-sweetened foods at all.

This book is to help you to understand the complex world of sugar so that you can begin to acknowledge and then reduce the amount of refined sugar that you eat. This does not mean you have to eat dull, tasteless food, on the contrary,

[1] The British Nutrition Foundation Task Force Report 1986.

recipes using whole (unrefined) foods have a natural sweetness and a delicious variety of tastes and textures.

The recipes are simple and inexpensive and you'll find your old-time favourites just as tasty, but with healthier ingredients. There are several chapters catering for the young where good eating habits should begin and lots of practical suggestions that have been successful in my family.

Finally, I've compiled a list of the more popular brands and own label products that contain no added sugar, so that you can begin today to cut down on your sugar for a healthier future.

PART ONE

1.
SUGAR —
THE CONTROVERSIAL ADDITIVE

'Sugar is pleasant to eat, inexpensive, gives "instant" energy and helps the world economy' — all very good reasons why over 38kg of sugar is consumed by each person in an average household every year,[1] over half of which is taken in commercially prepared foods, drinks and confectionery.

BUT

Too much sugar in our food can harm our health. Refined sugar is called an 'empty' food because it contains no other nutritional value other than to provide us with instant energy, which we can easily obtain from other foods in a well-balanced diet.

Here are a few very good reasons why we should reduce the quantity and frequency of sugar consumption in our diet.

Dental Caries

Sugar is now considered to be one of the major causes of tooth decay. Some foods, especially sugar, encourage the bacteria (plaque) in our mouths to produce large quantities of acid. The acid erodes the tooth enamel and dental decay begins. Although quantity of sugar is important, the frequency of exposing the bacteria to acid producing foods is also relevant. The effect of eating a boiled sweet may last up to half an hour in the mouth after the sweet has been finished. If another sweet is then eaten the teeth will be under continual acid attack and permanent dental decay will result.

Obesity

Excess sugar in the diet is directly related to overweight problems in many, especially children, and this can bring its own problems later in life, both healthwise, and socially. The intake of energy-producing foods must balance with energy output, otherwise the excess is laid down in the body tissue.

[1] Ministry of Agriculture, Fisheries and Food, *Consumption Levels Enquiry* Annual Report.

Health Disorders

Sugar is broken down by the digestive system into its two main components, glucose and fructose. **Fructose** is absorbed slowly into the blood stream, but **glucose** is rapidly utilized by the body in the form of energy. To regulate this, the pancreas produces large quantities of insulin and the well-balanced digestive system is disrupted.

Diabetes: The excess production of insulin due to the high intake of refined sugars has been known to relate to the development of diabetes in susceptible people, but as yet there is no clear evidence of a direct association between sugar consumption and this disease.

Allergies: A few people, especially children, have been found to react adversely to the intake of cane and beet sugars.

Addiction: The rise in the blood sugar level resulting from large quantities of sugar being absorbed may be experienced by some as an 'energy high'. This is rapidly followed by a 'low' and a craving for more sweet food results.

Malnutrition: Initial hunger feelings that are temporarily satisfied with a food high in sugar may result in loss of appetite for nutritional food. This is particularly important in the diet of young children.

Refined sugar needs vitamins from the B group to aid in its digestion and as these have all been removed from the sugar during refining, the body's own reserves will be drawn on, possibly causing a vitamin deficiency.

2.

A BRIEF HISTORY
OF REFINED SUGARS

It is unlikely that early man would have suffered the effects of too much sugar in his diet. His only source of sweetness coming from fruit and honey, over indulgence would have been hindered by the difficulties in collecting it.

Up to the 16th century only a very little sugar was being produced from cane, and this refined sugar remained expensive and scarce until the 19th century, when it quickly became more plentiful and less expensive, no doubt gaining in popularity along with tea and coffee. Originally, all refined sugar came from cane, but today this only accounts for about one-third of the sugar used, the larger proportion being from beet.

Since 1945 the sugar industry has rapidly expanded with sugar consumption in Britain at its maximum during the 1950's and 1960's. Over the past decade there has been considerable concern over the effect of so much sugar in our diet and the consumption of refined sugar is reported to have declined by 18 per cent.[1] However, this fall seems to relate only to the number of packets sold by the retailers as the quantity of sugar being used by the food industry has increased. There is a steady rise in the sale of confectionery (reported to be the highest amongst the EEC countries) and an even greater rise in the sale of soft drinks which has more than doubled in the last 30 years.[2] With the aim of reducing sugar consumption by half during the next 15 years, manufacturers have been requested to research new ways to sweeten food and re-formulate their products. This anticipated reduction in the use of refined sugars has, in its turn, made an extensive scientific research programme necessary to find alternative non-food uses for sugar to ensure a stable balance in the world economy.

---

[1] Information taken from a report on *Sugar Consumption in Britain* by A. J. Rugg-Gunn, RD, BDS, PhD, FDS, 1986.
[2] NACNE recommendation (National Advisory Committee on Nutrition Education) 1983.

3.
WHAT IS SUGAR?

Sugar is found naturally in all green plants and trees, being manufactured in their leaves and used as a source of energy. Some plants and trees have additional resources and these are used by the sugar industries to manufacture a vast range of sugars and syrups.

Sucrose

Most commonly referred to as 'refined' sugar, it is the cheapest and most plentiful type used in the Western World, yet it is thought to be the most harmful to our teeth, because of its 'stickiness'. Sucrose is used in vast quantities by the food industry. There are two main sources of sucrose:

(A) Cane sugar

The cane is crushed, boiled and washed several times until the sucrose is left pure and white.

Brown Sugar

e.g. Muscovado, Barbados — This is obtained after the first washing when the sugar crystals are still coated with brown sticky molasses. The country of origin should be printed on the packet which indicates it is genuine. Commercial brown sugars are made by re-colouring white sugar with molasses or colouring.

Syrup

This is the residue left after sugar refining. The colour and quality depends on the stage at which it was collected. Molasses (treacle) is the most concentrated.

(B) Beet sugar

The sucrose is obtained from the root of this plant by slicing, pulping, soaking and washing. Beet sugar is identical in strength and quality to cane, but brown sugars and syrups are not generally produced.

Palm Sugar

This is made from the sap of trees such as date and coconut. The clear syrup obtained from boiling the sap is crystallized.

Maple Syrup

The sap extracted from the maple tree is heated and reduced by boiling to give its depth of colour. Genuine maple syrup is expensive and has a distinctive flavour.

Fructose

Fructose (fruit sugar) occurs naturally in all fruit and vegetables. It can be isolated and refined into crystals and has a sweetness three times greater than sucrose. Although refined fructose is as harmful to our health and teeth as other sugars, when occurring in its natural state the concentration is low so less is eaten. Fructose is also absorbed more slowly into the blood stream than sucrose.

Lactose

This is the sugar occurring naturally in milk and therefore all dairy produce. It is less sweet and consumed in less concentration than other sugars.

Glucose/Dextrose

Sucrose can be broken down into glucose and fructose and this occurs naturally during digestion. Glucose is absorbed rapidly into the blood stream and it is often isolated and taken on its own to produce 'instant' energy.

Other Sugars/Syrups

Corn Syrup

This is derived from corn starch and is less sweet than cane and beet sugar. It is mainly used in the confectionery industry.

Starch Sugars — Glucose Syrup

These are a complex range of syrups produced from cereals and potatoes for the food industry.

N.B. *Poly-dextrose* is processed from starch and now used frequently as bulk with a sweetener in diabetic food products. It does not rate as sugar.

Malt Extract

A dark, sweet tasting syrup made from germinated and roasted grains rich in proteins, minerals and vitamins and often prescribed as a tonic. It contains maltose (malt sugar).

Honey

A partly-digested complex sugar broken down into glucose and fructose by the bee. It is therefore more easily assimilated by the body than sucrose, but should still be used sparingly. Honey contains a high percentage of water and its traces of vitamins are so small as to be insignificant in the diet. Honey varies considerably in flavour, colour and texture depending on the location of the hives.

Sweeteners

Over the past few years several non-sugar and artificial sweeteners have been produced, initially for the slimming market, but more recently they have gained popularity in the food industry as a direct result of the concern by the medical profession over our high consumption of sugar. These sweeteners can be derivatives of natural foods, or purely synthetic. There are numerous brands on the market including:

Sorbitol: Found naturally in some ripe fruit but produced commercially from sucrose or starch. 50 per cent as sweet as sugar and absorbed slowly. It is used widely in 'sugar-free' products and at present considered to be less cariogenic than sugar.

Mannitol: Found naturally in some vegetables. 50 per cent as sweet as sugar and slowly absorbed. Expensive.

Xylitol: Found naturally in some fruits and equals sucrose in sweetness. Commercially produced from birch trees. It does not produce acid in the mouth or raise blood sugar levels. Used in chewing gum and other confectioneries, ice cream and some medicines.

Intense Sweeteners

These are many hundreds of times sweeter than sucrose. Many are entirely synthetic and should be considered as an additive. Care should be taken in their use, especially in food for young children. Among the most popular sweeteners are:

Aspartame: Derived from amino-acids (protein) and is about 200 times sweeter than sugar. Sold in tablets for sweetening beverages. Non-acid forming in the mouth.

Saccharine: An organic salt. 300 times as sweet as sugar, but has an unpleasant after taste. Therefore often used with other sweeteners. Non-acid forming.

Cyclamate: 25 times as sweet as sugar used extensively in soft drinks and restricted in some countries including UK.

4.

HIDDEN SUGARS

It would be simple if we could eliminate sugar from our diet just by not stirring it into tea and coffee, or by giving up the daily bar of chocolate. Unfortunately sugar in this form accounts for only about 50 per cent of our sugar intake, the rest is commonly referred to as 'hidden sugar' because one is not always aware that it is being eaten. Manufacturers add sugar to nearly every product, both sweet and savoury. A plate of baked beans, sausages and ketchup (catsup) might contain nearly the same amount of sugar as your dessert.

Why do manufacturers add so much sugar? Partly for its chemical, physical and preserving qualities, but mainly for flavour which may contribute to the acceptability of certain foods. Some manufacturers claim that if they omitted sugar from baked beans, nobody would enjoy them, thus depriving many, both old and young, of a highly nutritious food.

Perhaps one of the most controversial areas of added sugar is in the baby food market. Many mothers are hoodwinked into believing that the 'experts' know best and with all the added vitamins these handy little jars must be better than home-cooked food. Now there is an area of doubt as mothers are being made aware of the actual contents of the jars. In the past baby food was often flavoured to suit the mother's taste and although salt and artificial additives are now banned, many varieties still contain an unnecessary high percentage of sugar. Even low-sugar teething rusks contain about ½ teaspoon of sugar per rusk, necessary, the manufacturers claim, to produce the dry, firm texture.

There has also been a lot of discussion recently on the numerous syrup-based vitamin enriched baby drinks — even when diluted these are far sweeter than necessary and the mis-interpretation of the 'daily dosage' can cause considerable damage. Soft and fizzy drinks for older children have a very high sugar content, too. Medicines, especially those designed for children, are syrup-based and can cause considerable harm to teeth if treatment is prolonged.

In line with modern day thinking, many food manufacturers are now having to re-develop their products to produce a range that is acceptable in flavour, quality and appearance, yet at the same time free from artificial additives, low in salt and free from added sugar.

Those who crave peaches in heavy syrup will now have to hunt for them, finding instead a vast range of 'fruit in natural juice'. Many products, especially baby foods now have a 'no added sugar' flash and one brand of baked beans proudly announce '50 per cent less sugar'.

The British Nutrition Foundation (April 1985) recommend 'the development of alternative products with a lower potential cariogenicity should be considered despite the costs of approved raw materials, research, development and marketing'. It goes on to stress that the promotion and marketing of these products should not mislead. If an established product has been re-formulated to contain less sucrose the advertising should not suggest that the final sugar content is substantially reduced if this is not the case. No added sucrose may still mean the product has a substantial sugar content. A good example is the Health Snack Bar. Very often they contain glucose, honey, raw cane sugar or fructose.

By law, manufacturers now have to list the ingredients of their products. The foods are listed in decreasing order of weight or percentage and thus one would expect to find the name of the product first on the list. This is not always so and water and sugar are often high on the list. We should make a habit of studying the ingredients before purchasing and care must be taken to recognize the various names for sugar. Generally speaking, words ending in 'ose' are sugar — dextrose, glucose, sucrose, glucose syrup, maltose, fructose. Honey, raw cane sugar, corn syrup and molasses are all sugars, too.

CAUTION Many 'sugar-free', 'sugar-reduced' or low calorie products contain another form of sweetener (see page 18) and you may wish to restrict your intake of these products, too.

5.

GENERAL HINTS FOR
REDUCING SUGAR IN THE DIET

It would be impractical to suggest that one should suddenly remove all refined sugar from the diet, not only because it would be virtually impossible, but our palates could not adjust to the new taste overnight. A gradual 'weaning' process away from sugary foods is a more practical suggestion and here are a few hints to help you re-educate your family towards a healthier, less sweet diet.

1. The obvious place to start is the packet of refined sugars (including raw cane) that you purchase each week. Use it more sparingly and try to lengthen the period between each purchase. Don't add sugar to beverages or cereal — in fact don't have a sugar bowl at all. Sweeten stewed fruit after cooking and cut down on those sticky, syrup-drenched puddings and cakes. Only 'ice' cakes for special occasions.

2. Change to unrefined wholefoods which are naturally sweeter and healthier, and because of their bulk make it difficult to over-eat. It would take some time to chew through a 3 foot (1 metre) length of sugar cane, yet takes only seconds to eat the one teaspoon of refined sugar that same piece of cane would yield if processed. Wholefoods also contain the necessary vitamins to help the body break down the sugar.

3. Switch to plainer cakes, and biscuits, but don't just replace sugar with honey or raw cane sugars — these are still highly concentrated forms of sugar. Instead, utilize the natural sweetness of fruit.

4. Only use commercial products on the odd occasion. With modern kitchen gadgets to do the preparations, home cooking isn't the lengthy chore it used to be, and it's far more nutritious.

5. Start young. Encourage your baby to enjoy plain and savoury foods rather than introducing him to highly-sweetened foods.

6. Sweets should not be used as bribes, rewards or passifiers and buying them with pocket money should be discouraged.

7. Make full use of the free range of information leaflets supplied by leading retailers detailing the nutritional content of their products. Don't be persuaded or misled by advertising or promotional gimmicks. Read each product label before buying. Remember, sugar comes in many guises.

6.

A PRACTICAL GUIDE
FOR A LOW-SUGAR DIET

The following chart can be used as a quick reference when planning meals or shopping lists. A more detailed list of commercial products containing no added sugar or having a sugar-reduced content are listed on page 145.

More details about home-made alternatives are under the various chapter headings.

* Avoid these products
** Use these products sparingly   *Alternative suggestions*

Drinks

Sugar added to tea/coffee/bed-time drinks/drinking chocolate.

1. Cut down on number of cups drunk.
2. Use non-nutritive sweeteners sparingly.

* Syrup-based squashes, cordials. Soft drinks/fizzy drinks.

1. Use mineral water or unsweetened fruit juices.
2. Squeeze your own juices.
3. Make your own drinks by liquidizing raw fruit and/or raw vegetables, sieving and slackening with water.
4. Liven up drinks with natural sparkling mineral water.

** Alcoholic drinks.

1. Make fruit punches with unsweetened fruit juices, fresh fruit and liven up with soda, mineral or tonic water and a sprig of fresh herbs.

*_Avoid these products_
**_Use these products sparingly_   _Alternative suggestions_

* Milk shakes and flavoured drinks.

1. Place fresh, soft-fruit and chilled, semi-skimmed milk in a blender. Don't add sugar, honey, food colouring or any sweeteners.

Breakfast Foods

* Chocolate, honey or sugar-coated refined cereal. Check ingredient list on muesli-type cereals. Many contain honey and sugars.

1. Buy wholegrain cereals.
2. Make your own muesli using wholegrains, nuts, wheatgerm, bran, dried fruit, etc.
3. Serve cereal with stewed or fresh fruit instead of sugar.

* Marmalade, preserves.

1. Use low-salt yeast or vegetable extracts, spreads or sugar-free peanut butter.
2. Choose 'sugar-reduced' preserves whenever possible.

Lunch

** Packet and canned soups.

1. Use vegetable stock, beans, pulses and fresh vegetables to make delicious homemade soups.
2. Liquidize tomatoes, celery, carrots or other fresh vegetables for refreshing 'instant' cold soups.

* Delicatessen meats, sausages, canned or prepacked meats, meat pies.

1. Replace with egg, cheese, beans, pulses, nuts and vegetables.

* Sauces, chutneys, pickles.

1. Use natural (plain) yogurt or low-fat cream cheese flavoured with fresh herbs, spices or a dash of tabasco or soy(a) sauce.
2. Use puréed tomatoes or cooked vegetables, 'spiced' up.

* ***Avoid these products***
** ***Use these products sparingly***   ***Alternative suggestions***

** Canned vegetables.

1. Fresh or frozen are better.

* Packet desserts and toppings.
Canned and frozen desserts.

1. Serve fresh fruit, natural (plain) yogurts, stewed fruit or low-sugar desserts (see page 109).
2. Finish meal with a piece of cheese to help clear mouth of sugary deposits.

* Fruit-flavoured jelly.

1. Use fresh fruit in unsweetened fruit juice set with agar agar or other vegetable setting gel.

* Fruit-flavoured yogurt.

1. Make your own and serve with fresh fruit, fruit purée, nuts, or dried fruit.
2. Choose varieties with no added sugar or artificial additives.

* Sweet sauces and flavoured syrups.

1. Use fresh fruit or fruit purée.

* Canned and pre-whipped creams.

1. Replace with natural (plain) yogurt, Greek or thick-set yogurt or evaporated milk used sparingly.

* Condensed milk (50 per cent sugar).

1. Replace as for cream.

** Ice-cream and fancy iced desserts.

1. Make your own using less sugar.

* Canned fruit in syrup.

1. Use fresh fruit whenever possible.
2. Choose canned fruit in 'natural' juice.

** Packet, canned or dried custard.

1. Make your own sauce using milk and eggs.
2. Replace as for cream.

* *Avoid these products*
** *Use these products sparingly*   *Alternative suggestions*

Tea Time

* Jams, syrup, honey, commercial
spreads.

1. Use unsweetened peanut butter.
2. Low-salt vegetable or yeast
   extracts/spreads.
3. Pear 'n Apple Spread, use
   sparingly.
4. Make your own fruit butters by
   reducing stewed fruit to thick
   consistency or mashing soft fruit
   or softened dried fruit into low-
   fat cream cheese or sieved
   cottage cheese.
5. Select from range of low-sugar
   jams.

** Malt and currant breads. Fancy
sweet breads and teacakes.

1. Use wholemeal (wheat) or mixed
   grain breads.

* Rich chocolate or cream-filled
cakes, fancy cakes, rich fruit cakes.

1. Make your own using
   wholemeal (wheat) flour and less
   sugar (see chapter on Family
   Cakes page 94).
2. Select plain cakes without icing
   or jam.

** Glacéed fruits.

1. Use dried, fresh or canned fruits.

** Marzipan.

1. Low-sugar almond paste (see
   page 131).

* Sugar-coated cake decorations.

1. Chopped nuts, sunflower,
   sesame or other seeds.

** Chocolate.

1. Replace with carob flour or
   carob block for grating,
   chopping or melting.

Snacks

* Chocolate-coated or cream-filled
biscuits.

1. Buy savoury biscuits, crackers,
   bread sticks or rice biscuits.
2. Make your own using reduced
   sugar or flavour with cheese.

Avoid these products
Use these products sparingly   *Alternative suggestions*

** Health bars.

1. Read list of ingredients first or make your own.

* Commercial snacks.

1. Make your own popcorn — add no sugar or salt.
2. Eat nuts, fresh fruit or sticks of raw salad vegetables, dried fruit.

* Sweets, especially sticky, chewy or lingering sweets.

1. Offer alternatives (see chapter on Toddler's Teeth, page 46).

Baby Foods

* Vitamin-enriched syrups.

1. Use well-diluted unsweetened fruit juice, freshly squeezed juice or cooled, boiled water or milk.
2. Serve plenty of fresh fruit and vegetables.
3. Use vitamin drops (check with Health Visitor).

** Commercially prepared jars, tins and packets of baby food.

1. Use only occasionally.
2. Serve freshly cooked food whenever possible.

* Teething Rusks.

1. Use thick fingers of wholemeal (wheat) bread dried out in a cool oven.
2. Sticks of carrot or celery.
3. Bickiepegs.

General

** Syrup-based medicines especially over long periods.

1. Ask at the chemist for 'sucrose-free' medicine.
2. Transfer children to junior tablets for minor ailments (check with pharmacist).

* Glucose tablets or sweets.

1. Eat a balanced diet including unrefined carbohydrates for fitness and energy.

7.
ABOUT THE RECIPES

The Chapters are divided into age groups and situations rather than types of food, i.e. Weaning, Toddler's food, Teenage Party, Packed Lunches, Family Cakes and Puddings, Entertaining and Seasonal Fare. Obviously many of these recipes are interchangeable, and you will find a cross reference on page 153.

The Recipes use wholefood ingredients which are naturally sweeter, many of which you will be able to buy at the supermarket. There are a few ingredients you will not find there yet, and these can be obtained from Boots the Chemist or any health food shop or counter. For readers less familiar with these products I have added notes in the Ingredient Guide on page

'Sweetness'. Remember you should re-educate your palate by slowly reducing the sweetness. Many of the recipes contain no added sweetener relying on the natural sweetness of the ingredients used. Readers with a desire for highly sweetened food may wish to add a little sweetener at first, slowly reducing the quantity used. Don't use honey or sucrose in any form, instead add very small quantities of fructose or a few drops of Apple Concentrate. Try not to dictate your palate to the rest of the family, especially the young, who may enjoy a recipe that you, at first, find unacceptable.

Fruit. Experiment and vary the fruit used in the early chapters, making full use of fresh fruit when available, relying on dried or canned fruit in natural juice when the various fruits are out of season. The 'sweetness' of any recipes will vary according to the type and ripeness of the fruit used.

In the latter recipes, a few drops of lemon juice or a pinch of ground spice will help to sharpen up the flavour if you find it too bland.

Butter, Cream, Milk etc. Because of its excellent flavour, the natural product butter has been used in these recipes. However, vegetable margarine may be substituted, if desired. Similarly, low-fat products may replace cream cheese and yogurts but care should be taken when adding liquid to these recipes as the consistency may be affected by low-fat products (see Ingredient Guide). Use skimmed milk where preferred except for toddlers who will benefit from the nutrients in whole milk.

8.
INGREDIENT GUIDE

Available from most large supermarkets:

Flour

Wholemeal (wheat) 100 per cent extraction — has nothing added or taken away. Available plain or self-raising, although latter may be difficult to find. Stoneground is coarser.

Brown (Wheatmeal) 81 per cent extraction — coarser particles removed. Some people may prefer its texture for pastry and it may be substituted in these recipes.

Fruit Juice — Unsweetened

Not to be confused with 'fruit drinks'. A variety of unsweetened fruit juices are available without preservatives from the chilled cabinet. Pineapple and apple are the sweetest. Also available, pure freshly squeezed orange and lemon juice.

Fruits — Canned in 'Natural Juice'

Usually grape or apple juice is used. Increasing variety of fruits now available, and although still fairly sweet, are considerably less so than those in syrup.

Fruits — Dried

Seek out those coated in 'vegetable oil' rather than 'food grade white mineral oil and preservatives'. Alternatively, buy from health food shops. 'Ready to use' are more expensive, but need less soaking. Apricots and the vine fruits are the sweetest.

Nuts

Buy shelled nuts with their skins left on. Peanuts and cashews usually available from the snack section, other nuts from the baking section. Pecan and cashew nuts are the most expensive, but grind down well. Peanuts and hazelnuts tend to be the cheapest.

Yogurts — Natural (Plain)
Usually low-fat milk, but 'strained' yogurts can be made from either full-fat or low-fat milk. Greek 'strained' yogurt has a velvety consistency and can replace double cream in most recipes (except for whipping). Also available from ewe's milk but not so smooth.

Yogurts — Fruit
Most fruit and fruit-flavoured yogurts contain a high percentage of sugar and additives. Look for those that contain only added fruit and fruit juice.

Fructose
Refined fruit sugar which has been crystallized. It is 3 times sweeter than sucrose so use sparingly.

Creamed Coconut
Pure coconut in block form. Use by chopping or grating and stirring into hot liquid to melt. May be more easily found in a small, local shop selling a cosmopolitan range of food products.

Cream (Soft) Cheese
Available from full-fat or low-fat milk. 'Soft' cheese made from skimmed milk is similar to curd or the continental 'Quark' cheese (see pages 27 and 134).

Available from Health Food Shops or Counters within Food Halls

Brown Rice
Whole unpolished grains of rice containing large amounts of vitamins, minerals and protein. Available as long or short grain, but takes longer to cook than polished white rice.

Brown Rice Flakes
Whole unpolished grains of rice processed into flakes. Cooks more quickly than whole grains. Use also to thicken sauces and cooked fruit purées.

Wheatgerm
Part of the wheat grain rich in protein. It can be stirred into fruit purées, to thicken.

Wholemeal (wheat) Semolina
Particles of wheat grain (endosperm) with the bran.

Wheatflakes
Crushed wholewheat grains not to be confused with the processed cereal flakes.

Carob Powder/Block
Made from pods of the carob tree and manufactured to resemble cocoa powder in appearance and is used as a substitute in cooking. Carob is naturally sweeter, contains more nutrients and is caffeine-free. Also available in block form for eating, grating or melting for use in cooking. Some varieties have no added sugar and contain the natural oils of fruit for flavouring.

Vegetable Setting Gel
Gelatine substitute made from seaweed. Agar agar, Carageen and brand products. Has a greater setting power than gelatine.
   N.B. Agar agar has been used in these recipes.

Low-Salt Yeast Extract
Various brand names — no added salt e.g. Natex.

Vegetable Stock or Spread
Various brand names — no added salt e.g. Vecon.

Pear 'n Apple Spread
A thick sweetish spread made from concentrated pears and apples. Replaces jam, but use sparingly. There are two varieties, namely Sunwheel and Whole Earth's Pear and Apple Pure Fruit Spread.

Apple Concentrate
Highly concentrated apple juice. Use sparingly to sweeten or glaze food, or as a drink, well diluted.

Nuts and Seeds
A large range of nuts and seeds are available.

'Live' Yogurt
These yogurts contain bacteria beneficial to health.

Sweet Cicely
A fern-like herb that helps to reduce tartness if cooked with fruit. Sometimes sold as seedlings, or seek out at your gardening centre.

Vegetable Margarine
Available as soft spread or hard for baking. It contains no animal product, gluten, lactose, colour or added flavour.

9.
CONVERSION CHARTS

Imperial/Metric Conversion Tables

¼ oz	7g	9 oz	255g
½ oz	15g	10 oz	285g
¾ oz	20g	11 oz	310g
1 oz	30g	¾ lb	340g
2 oz	55g	13 oz	370g
3 oz	85g	14 oz	395g
4 oz	115g	15 oz	425g
5 oz	140g	1 lb	455g
6 oz	170g	1¼ lb	565g
7 oz	200g	1½ lb	680g
½ lb	225g	2 lb	900g

Liquids

Imperial	Metric	Fluid Ounces	American
—	30ml	1 fl oz	2 tablespoons
—	60ml	2 fl oz	¼ cup
—	90ml	3 fl oz	⅓ cup
¼ pint	140ml	5 fl oz	⅔ cup
⅓ pint	200ml	7 fl oz	¾ cup
½ pint	285ml	10 fl oz	1⅓ cups
⅔ pint	340ml	12 fl oz	1½ cups
¾ pint	425ml	15 fl oz	2 cups
1 pint	570ml	20 fl oz	2½ cups
1½ pints	850ml	30 fl oz	3¾ cups

NB.
British Standard cup = 10 fl oz
American Standard cup = 8 fl oz

Follow either imperial, metric or American measurements only. Do not mix them.

Spoons: All measurements are level.
1 teaspoon = 5ml
1 tablespoon = 15ml

Oven Temperatures

Gas Mark	Centigrade	Fahrenheit	Heat Level
¼	110	225	very cool
½	130	250	very cool
1	140	275	cool or slow
2	150	300	cool or slow
3	170	325	warm
4	180	350	moderate
5	190	375	moderately hot
6	200	400	fairly hot
7	220	425	hot
8	230	450	very hot
9	240	475	very hot

Opposite: From Weaning section: Fruit Salad (page 40), Spring Salad (page 42), Baked Egg Custard (page 44).

Overleaf: From Toddler's Teeth section: Strawberry Shake (page 56), Popcorn (page 50), Apple Flake Pudding (page 52).

PART TWO
The Recipes

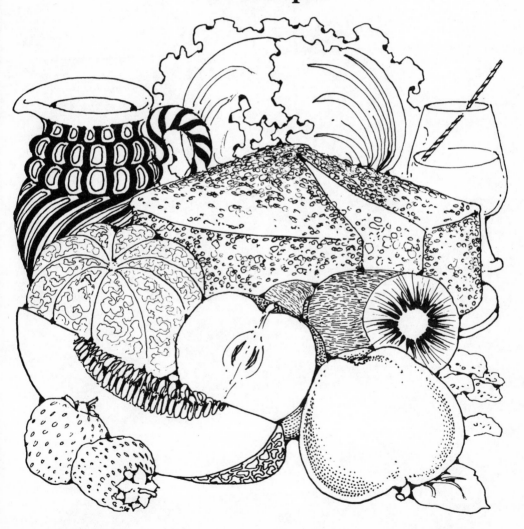

1.

WEANING

Your baby's tastebuds are not yet fully developed, so now is the time to ensure that he doesn't develop a desire for sweet foods.

Baby Foods
Although vitamin-enriched, these contain a high percentage of water, starch and sugar so only use them occasionally.

Family Meals
Most of the family meals you cook yourself are suitable for baby (except fried foods) but it is wise to add the seasoning at the end of cooking time after removing baby's portion. When you have time it is worth making up a special 'baby' dish for freezing in small portions such as in the ice cube tray. When frozen, store the cubes in a labelled bag or box for up to 6 weeks to ensure a good rotation. Leave cubes to thaw slowly in fridge.

Fruit and Vegetables
Use raw whenever possible to make a purée and thicken, if necessary, with wheatgerm. If using a blender it isn't necessary to remove skins, but do remember to wash them first. Fruit to be cooked can be baked or poached whole, after piercing the skin, to help retain the nutrients.

The sweetness of fruit depends on the degree of ripeness and dessert fruit, e.g. apples, are sweeter than the cooking varieties, but don't break down so readily. When fresh fruit is unobtainable, use frozen or canned fruit in natural juices. Frozen vegetables are preferable to the canned varieties, which often contain salt, sugar and sometimes colouring.

Wholefood Diet
Serve the kind of diet you intend to continue, but don't overload with too much roughage. Leave the skins on fruit and vegetables and only remove if there is a danger of choking. Remember that if you only give your child wholemeal(wheat)

bread, he'll not take a preference for white, likewise with natural (plain) yogurt versus the fruit-flavoured ones.

Teething Rusks
Recent reports have shown that even the 'low-sugar' rusks contain up to ½ teaspoon of sugar each. So use Bickiepegs or hard-baked fingers of bread.

Drinks
Most vitamin-enriched baby drinks are syrup-based and even when diluted are far sweeter than is necessary. The 'daily-dosage' warnings are often misleading, too. Your baby should be getting sufficient vitamin C if you are serving plenty of fresh fruit and vegetables. If in doubt, ask your Health Visitor about vitamin drops.

Cooled, boiled water is the best drink and never leave anything else for night-time thirst. Freshly-squeezed orange juice, homemade fruit and vegetable juices (well-strained) or well-diluted unsweetened fruit juice are suitable.

CAUTION:
Never put anything else but milk or water in a baby's feeding bottle. Introduce fruit juice in a drinking cup or help your baby drink from a small egg cup or teaspoon so he doesn't suck continually on fruit juice throughout the day.

Messy But Happy
Encourage baby to feed himself as soon as possible. Sit him up at the table with the rest of the family and he'll soon get the message that eating can be fun — and messy! Invest in a large plastic apron with sleeves, the kind sold for children's painting, and he'll need a pelican bib, too. Give him a teaspoon and he's all set to go.

Serve finger foods as well as the main meal — a few small cubes of cheese or bread, cooked peas, carrots or pasta shapes can all be placed by the side of the bowl.

Remember your baby is used to a 4-hourly routine — so don't keep him waiting. Far better than curbing his appetite with drinks or biscuits.

Allergies
Only a few babies develop an allergy to certain foods. Those that can cause temporary difficulties are wheat (gluten), milk, orange, egg and cane or beet sugar. It is therefore wise to introduce the different foods slowly on a rotation basis. Consult your doctor or Health Visitor if in doubt.

Rusks

These can be made whenever you have the oven in use. Turn the oven down to cool, 250°F/130°C (Gas Mark ½).

Imperial/Metric
½ inch (1.3cm) thick slices of wholemeal bread

American
½ inch thick slices of wholewheat bread

1. Cut bread into ¾ inch (2cm) wide fingers and place on a baking sheet.

2. Place in the oven for about 1 hour until rusks are dried out and hard.

3. When cold, store in an airtight tin.

Variation:

Savoury Rusks

For each slice of bread:

Imperial/Metric
¼ teaspoon low-salt yeast or vegetable extract/spread
4 tablespoons hot water or milk

American
¼ teaspoon low-salt yeast or vegetable extract/spread
4 tablespoons hot water or milk

1. Cut bread as above.

2. Dissolve yeast or vegetable extract in the hot water or milk and pour into a shallow dish.

3. Add bread fingers and turn them gently over to absorb the liquid.

4. Carefully transfer fingers to a greased baking sheet and bake as above. They will take up to 2 hours to dry.

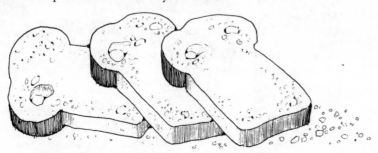

Breakfast Muesli

Use a blender or food processor to grind the ingredients and vary the fineness according to the age of the baby.

Suggested Ingredients

Imperial/Metric	**American**
2 rounded tablespoons rolled oats	2 rounded tablespoons rolled oats
1 teaspoon wheatgerm	1 teaspoon wheatgerm
1 teaspoon desiccated or flaked coconut	1 teaspoon desiccated or flaked coconut
1 tablespoon wheatflakes	1 tablespoon wheatflakes
1 tablespoon raisins or sultanas	1 tablespoon raisins or golden seedless raisins

1. Place all ingredients into a blender or food processor and run machine until fruit is finely chopped.

2. Store in a screw-top jar in the fridge.

To serve:
Mix 1 teaspoon (or more according to age) of muesli with a little warm milk/boiled water to make a soft paste. Leave 5 minutes. Just before serving stir in a little finely grated apple or pear and a little natural (plain) yogurt or fresh orange juice.

Variation:
Any dried fruit such as dates, apricots, or 'ready-to-use' prunes may be used instead of raisins.

Warm Starter

As many baby cereals have added sugar, make sure you read the list of ingredients first before buying.

Imperial/Metric	**American**
3 rounded tablespoons unsweetened baby rice cereal	3 rounded tablespoons unsweetened baby rice cereal
¼ teaspoon bran	¼ teaspoon bran
1 dessertspoon sultanas, chopped dates or dried apricots	2 teaspoons golden seedless raisins, chopped dates or dried apricots

1. Place ingredients in a blender or food processor and run machine until fruit is finely chopped.

2. Store in a screw-top jar in the fridge.

To serve:
Make up the rice cereal as directed on the packet using milk or water. Add a little finely grated apple or pear just before serving.

Apple and Carrot Juice

Ideally the home-made juices should be used immediately, but it's difficult to make small quantities. Alternatively, make large quantities and serve to the family.

Imperial/Metric	American
1 dessert apple, washed, cored and chopped	1 dessert apple, washed, cored and chopped
1 small carrot, scrubbed and grated	1 small carrot, scrubbed and grated

1. Place apple and carrot in a blender or liquidizer with ¼ pint (140ml/⅔ cup) water or sufficient to make machine run easily and make a smooth purée.

2. Serve immediately or freeze in ice cube trays, for up to 7 days.

To serve:
Dilute purée with ¼ pint (140ml/⅔ cup) water and strain through wet muslin. Dilute to taste.

Note: The undiluted purée can be served on its own or stirred into baby cereal or Breakfast Muesli.

Alternatives:
Try any combination of the following to make healthy drinks for baby and yourself: apple, celery, carrot, orange, tomato, pineapple, pear, soft summer fruits.

Fruit Salad

These are best used immediately, but you will have to make sufficient for your liquidizer (blender) to run smoothly. Use fresh fruit when available.

Imperial/Metric	American
2 tablespoons chopped dried apricots or peaches	2 tablespoons chopped dried apricots or peaches
1 dessert apple	1 dessert apple
Few drops lemon juice	Few drops lemon juice
3-4 tablespoons unsweetened fruit juice	3-4 tablespoons unsweetened fruit juice

1. Cover dried fruit with water and leave to soak overnight or until soft. Drain.

2. Wash and core apple but don't peel. Roughly chop and place in a liquidizer (blender) with the apricots or peaches, lemon juice and sufficient fruit juice to allow the machine to run smoothly.

3. Blend well until skin is very finely chopped.

4. Use same day or place immediately in ice cube tray and freeze. Store up to 7 days.

To serve:
On its own or with natural (plain) yogurt. Stir in a little wheatgerm to thicken, if necessary.

Apple Purée

Any thick-skinned fruit can be cooked like this whenever you are using the oven.

Imperial/Metric	American
1 cooking apple	1 cooking apple
2 dates, stoned	2 dates, pitted
Small knob of butter	Small knob of butter
Few drops apple concentrate	Few drops apple concentrate

1. Wash apple and remove core. Cut through skin round apple and place dates in the centre hole. Wrap apple loosely in foil and place in a dish containing 1 inch (2.5cm) water.

2. Cook in a moderate oven 350°F/180°C (Gas Mark 4) for about 45 minutes until soft.

3. Carefully unwrap apple, discard skin and sieve pulp and dates together. Stir in butter and a few drops of apple concentrate to remove tartness, if desired.

Storage:
Freeze in ice cube tray for up to 3 months.

To serve:
Warm or cold with natural (plain) yogurt or breakfast cereal.

Spring Salad

Any salad vegetable can be given to a baby, but make sure it is finely chopped or puréed for easy digestion.

Imperial/Metric	American
½ tomato	½ tomato
½ baby beetroot, cooked	½ baby beetroot, cooked
2 inch (5cm) piece celery	2 inch stalk of celery
½ inch (1.3cm) slice of cucumber	½ inch slice of cucumber
2 oz (55g) lettuce heart	2 ounces lettuce heart

1. Roughly chop all ingredients and place in a blender or food processor and run machine until finely chopped or puréed as desired. Add a little extra tomato, if necessary, to make machine run smoothly.

Storage:
Best used same day or frozen immediately in ice cube tray.

To serve:
As a sauce over potatoes or rice, on its own, or with a few teaspoons of natural (plain) yogurt stirred in. Thicken with a little wheatgerm, if necessary.

Blackcurrant and Apple Dessert

This is an excellent way to serve blackcurrants, alternatively, the purée can be diluted and strained to use as a drink.

Imperial/Metric	American
1 oz (25g) blackcurrants	3 tablespoons blackcurrants
6 tablespoons unsweetened apple juice	6 tablespoons unsweetened apple juice
1 dessert apple	1 dessert apple
Wheatgerm, to thicken	Wheatgerm, to thicken

1. Place blackcurrants and apple juice in a small saucepan which has a tightly fitting lid.

2. Wash apple and discard core. Finely chop the apple and add to the pan. Cover and simmer gently for 3-4 minutes until blackcurrants are soft.

3. Liquidize the fruit and juice to make a smooth purée.

Storage:
Freeze in ice cube containers for up to 4 weeks.

To serve:
As a dessert on its own or with a cereal. Thicken with a little wheatgerm, if necessary.

Custard Sauce

A nourishing basic sauce to use with both sweet and savoury foods.

Imperial/Metric	**American**
¼ pint (140ml) milk/water	⅔ cup milk/water
1 egg yolk, beaten	1 egg yolk, beaten
4 teaspoons brown flaked rice	4 teaspoons brown flaked rice

1. Warm milk, then slowly pour onto yolk, stirring continuously.

2. Return milk to pan, sprinkle in flaked rice and stir over a low heat for 4-5 minutes until mixture thickens. Liquidize until smooth, if desired.

Storage:
Covered in the fridge up to 24 hours.

To serve:
Warm or cold with puréed fruit or vegetables.

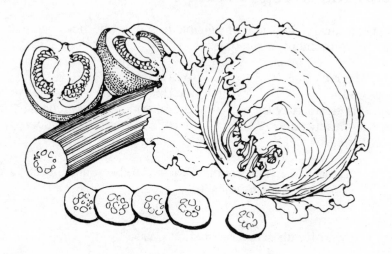

Baked Egg Custard

This can be made whenever you have the oven on moderate to low. Alternatively, stand cup in a tin or saucepan and cook slowly over a burner. Egg custards also cook well in the microwave oven on a low setting but need careful watching when such a small quantity is cooked.

Imperial/Metric
¼ pint (140ml) milk/water
2 small egg yolks

American
⅔ cup milk/water
2 small egg yolks

1. Place ½ inch (1.3cm) hot water in an ovenproof dish.

2. Lightly whisk milk and yolks together. Strain into a cup or small basin and cover with foil. Stand cup (basin) in prepared dish and bake below centre of oven for about 30 minutes or until just set.

3. Carefully remove from oven, cool, then place in fridge several hours or overnight to become firm.

Storage:
2 days in fridge. Do not freeze.

To serve:
On its own or with puréed fruit or vegetables.

Avocado and Orange Cream

Avocado pears are a rich source of valuable nutrients but they need to be used at just the right moment of ripeness.

Imperial/Metric
¼ ripe avocado
2 tablespoons cream cheese
1 tablespoon freshly squeezed
  orange juice

American
¼ ripe avocado
2 tablespoons cream cheese
1 tablespoon freshly squeezed
  orange juice

1. Peel avocado and mash until smooth. Beat cream cheese and mix into avocado with a little orange juice to slacken.

To serve:
Serve on its own or with cereal or mashed potato.

Storage:
Place in a small pot and cover with cling film; store only a few hours in the fridge as it will darken gradually. Stir before use.

2.

TODDLERS' TEETH — KEEP THEM HEALTHY

Although a young child only keeps his milk teeth for a few years, it is very important to look after them to ensure the healthy growth of his secondary teeth which must last him throughout his life.

Frequent 'in-between meal' snacks should be discouraged, a habit often formed through boredom rather than hunger or thirst. It's a good idea to make a few firm rules as a guideline and try not to deviate, especially in the early days, so that a good healthy eating habit is formed.

Out and About
If you buy a packet of sweets or an ice-cream to eat one day, then you'll never be able to pass a sweetshop again without trouble. A 'special' banana chosen at the greengrocer and carried home in a bag can engender just as much excitement from a young child. It's a good idea to always carry your own diluted fruit juice in a suitable container, then you won't be faced with the option of having to buy a canned drink.

Children can be very persuasive when shopping, especially in a supermarket with a threat of an imminent tantrum. If you select two or three varieties of what *you* want to buy, such as canned fruit in natural juice, the children can still make a choice about which fruit they like. Packet cereals with promotional gimmicks and yogurts with their favourite characters on can be a problem, but initial selection by you can help. Alternatively let them choose one of their choice while you select the remainder. There's no need to buy fancy biscuits either; a hungry child will enjoy even a homemade baby's rusk if that's all he's offered. If you can resist the temptation to buy, then once home, there's no choice.

Sweets
It would be unfair to expect your child never to eat sweets because of the society in which we live. Again, decide exactly how strict you wish to be, but it isn't a good idea to forbid sweets altogether as this can lead to deceit in even the youngest child. It's better, too, to buy the sweets yourself rather than encourage the use of pocket money.

Sweets should never be used as a bribe, reward or comforter or offered to children as they come out of school. Either wait until you reach home before offering a snack, or if the journey is long or delayed an apple or a few nuts will be better. Whatever you do, avoid making a habit of giving sweets at set times or occasions. Even a baby will soon learn to expect them.

Sweets that can be eaten quickly are far better for teeth than those that linger, e.g. peppermints, toffees. Try also to encourage grandparents not to bring sweets; a coin for the moneybox or an old hat for the dressing up box will be received just as enthusiastically, and saves money, too.

Banana Ice Cream

Make this ice cream in ice cube containers or other suitable small pots.

Imperial/Metric	**American**
2 large ripe bananas	2 large ripe bananas
¼ pint (140ml) natural yogurt	⅔ cup plain yogurt
¼ pint (140ml) evaporated milk, chilled	⅔ cup evaporated milk, chilled

1. Peel and roughly chop bananas and place in a liquidizer (blender) with the yogurt and run machine until mixture is smooth. Alternatively mash bananas with a fork and beat in yogurt.

2. Place mixture in a suitable container in the freezer or ice making compartment until just beginning to freeze round edges.

3. Whisk evaporated milk until thick. Whisk yogurt mixture until smooth, then fold in evaporated milk.

4. Divide between small containers and cover with foil and freeze.

Storage:
Quickly remove from container if necessary, and store in labelled plastic bags up to 4 weeks.

To serve:
Place ice cream in fridge 15 to 20 minutes before serving.

Muesli

Imperial/Metric	**American**
2 tablespoons sesame seeds	2 tablespoons sesame seeds
2 tablespoons desiccated coconut	2 tablespoons desiccated coconut
1 oz (30g) shelled nuts, finely chopped	3 tablespoons shelled nuts, finely chopped
4 oz (115g) rolled oats	1 cup rolled oats
1 oz (30g) wheatflakes	⅔ cup wheatflakes
1 rounded tablespoon bran	1 rounded tablespoon bran
1 oz (30g) wheatgerm	¼ cup wheatgerm
3 oz (85g) mixed dried fruit, chopped, e.g. raisins, sultanas, apricots, bananas, pears, peaches, figs, dates	½ cup mixed dried fruit, chopped, e.g. raisins, golden seedless raisins, apricots, bananas, pears, peaches, figs, dates

1. Prepare a moderately hot grill (broiler) and line the pan with kitchen foil.

2. Mix sesame seeds, desiccated coconut and nuts together and spread over foil. Toast, turning occasionally until golden brown. Leave to cool.

3. Mix oats, wheatflakes, bran, wheatgerm, sesame seeds, coconut, nuts, and dried fruit together.

N.B. Younger children may prefer the mixture ground in a blender for a few seconds.

Storage:
Store in a screw-top jar or airtight plastic box in a cool place.

To serve:
Place one or more heaped tablespoons in a bowl and mix with a little hot milk. Leave to stand 2 to 3 minutes. Stir in a little natural (plain) yogurt or fresh fruit just before serving.

Fresh Fruit Salad

It is unnecessary to make a sugar syrup for a fruit salad. Finely chopped fruit is easy to eat and will encourage children to enjoy fruit.

Imperial/Metric	**American**
1 orange	1 orange
1 dessert apple	1 dessert apple
1 small banana	1 small banana
1 kiwi fruit, or grapes	1 kiwi fruit, or grapes
2 tablespoons unsweetened fruit juice	2 tablespoons unsweetened fruit juice

1. Cut away peel and then cut down between segments to release flesh from orange (hold over a bowl to catch juice). Chop flesh and place in a bowl.

2. Wash apple and cut into quarters, remove core and finely chop apple. Add to bowl and stir into orange, to coat with juice.

3. Peel and slice banana and kiwi fruit, or wash and halve grapes, discarding pips. Cut each piece into quarters and add to bowl with the fruit juice.

4. Lightly toss fruit then cover bowl with clingfilm.

5. Leave for 1 hour at room temperature before placing in fridge.

Storage:
Store up to 24 hours in fridge. Vary the fruit as necessary. Fresh fruit salad is unsuitable for freezing.

Popcorn

Follow the instructions on the packet or use this method. Don't add salt or sugar.

Imperial/Metric
2 tablespoons vegetable oil
2 tablespoons popping corn

American
2 tablespoons vegetable oil
2 tablespoons popping corn

1. Place the oil in a large heavy-based pan which has a tightly fitting lid. Heat oil until a light haze is seen.

2. Add corn, all at once, and quickly put on lid. Shake pan (holding lid and handle) several times over a high flame until 'popping' begins.

3. Remove pan from heat when popping ceases. Remove lid; turn popcorn into a dish. Serve warm or cold.

Variations:
While popcorn is still hot, it can be tossed in a little finely grated cheese or finely grated dessert carob.

Fruity Marbles

(Makes 20)

This mixture can be cut or moulded into various shapes, but keep them small.

Imperial/Metric
3 oz (85g) dates, stoned
2 oz (55g) sultanas
2 oz (55g) raisins
2 tablespoons ground almonds
1 teaspoon finely grated lemon or
    orange rind

American
½ cup dates, pitted
⅓ cup golden seedless raisins
⅓ cup raisins
2 tablespoons ground almonds
1 teaspoon finely grated lemon or
    orange rind

To coat:

Desiccated coconut, toasted sesame
    seeds, finely chopped nut

Desiccated coconut, toasted sesame
    seeds, finely chopped nut

1. Place dates, sultanas (golden seedless raisins), raisins, ground almonds and rind in a blender and run machine to make a thick paste (or pass through a mincer).

2. Chill mixture then shape into small marble-sized balls. Roll balls in one of the suggested coatings. Store in the fridge up to 7 days.

N.B. Offer instead of sweets and use accordingly.

Date Flaps

(Makes 49×1 inch/2.5cm squares)

Imperial/Metric	**American**
4 oz (115g) butter	1 stick (½ cup) butter
3 tablespoons malt extract	3 tablespoons malt extract
6 oz (170g) rolled oats	1½ cups rolled oats
1 oz (30g) dates, chopped	¼ cup chopped dates

1. Prepare a moderate oven 350°F/180°C (Gas Mark 4). Grease a 7 inch (18cm) square tin.

2. Place butter and malt extract in a saucepan over a low heat until butter has melted. Stir in oats and dates.

3. Press mixture into prepared tin. Bake 20 minutes. Cool in tin, then turn out onto a chopping board and cut into 1 inch (2.5cm) squares or thin fingers.

Storage:
In a tin or wrapped in foil for up to 10 days.

N.B. 4 tablespoons Pear 'n Apple Spread may be used instead of malt extract.

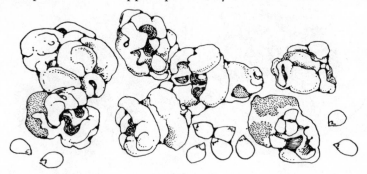

Apple Flake Pudding

(Makes 3-4 portions)

A quick, nourishing milk pudding that every member of the family will enjoy; just double the quantity.

Imperial/Metric	American
1 orange	1 orange
½ pint (285ml) milk	1⅓ cups milk
1½ oz (45g) brown flaked rice	8 tablespoons brown flaked rice
1 dessert apple	1 dessert apple
¼ pint (140ml) evaporated milk	⅔ cup evaporated milk

1. Wash orange and remove zest with a potato peeler. Place zest, milk and rice flakes in a small saucepan and bring slowly to the boil. Reduce heat and simmer, stirring occasionally for 2 to 3 minutes.

2. Wash and grate apple, add to pan and continue cooking a further 2-3 minutes, stirring, until mixture is thick.

3. Gradually stir in evaporated milk and cook until mixture coats back of spoon. Remove from heat and discard orange zest.

Storage:
Freeze in small containers for up to 6 weeks.

To serve:
Warm or cold with the orange flesh.

N.B. Do not boil once evaporated milk has been added, as it easily burns.

Blackcurrant and Apple Butter

(Makes about 1 lb/455g)

A thick purée of fruits to replace jam, but it cannot be stored for more than a week because of the low-sugar content.

Imperial/Metric
4 oz (115g) blackcurrants
½ lb (225g) chopped cooking apples
¼ pint (140ml) unsweetened apple juice
2 tablespoons apple concentrate
Juice of medium sized orange

American
¾ cup blackcurrants
1⅓ cups chopped cooking apples
⅔ cup unsweetened apple juice
2 tablespoons apple concentrate
Juice of medium sized orange

1. Sterilize a 1 lb (455g) jar and keep warm.

2. Place blackcurrants, apple and unsweetened apple juice in small pan, cover and cook over a low heat until fruit is soft.

3. Add apple concentrate and orange juice and simmer, uncovered for 10-15 minutes, stirring occasionally, until thick and pulpy. The purée is ready when the base of the saucepan can be seen as you stir. Be careful not to let the purée burn.

4. Pour purée into prepared jar and seal. Leave to cool.

Storage:
In the fridge up to one week.

To use:
On bread or in cooking instead of jam.

Variations:
Replace the blackcurrants with any variety of fruit, but keep the apple as this forms a good 'base'.

Apple Fool

(Serves 4-5)

Imperial/Metric
¾ lb (340g) prepared cooking apples, sliced
¼ pint (140ml) unsweetened orange or apple juice
Pinch of ground nutmeg or ginger
4 oz (115g) cream cheese
1 egg, separated
4 tablespoons thick set yogurt

American
2 cups prepared cooking apples, sliced
⅔ cup unsweetened orange or apple juice
Pinch of ground nutmeg or ginger
½ cup cream cheese
1 egg, separated
4 tablespoons thick set yogurt

1. Place apples, juice and spice in a small saucepan, cover with a tightly fitting lid and simmer gently until apples are soft. Purée and chill.

2. Beat cheese until smooth, gradually add egg yolk and yogurt. Stir in apple purée.

3. Whisk egg white until thick and fold into apple mixture. Divide between 4 or 5 small containers. Chill.

Storage:
2 days in fridge.

To serve:
Decorate with a little grated carob.

Variation:
Substitute one-third of the apple with blackcurrants or blackberries.

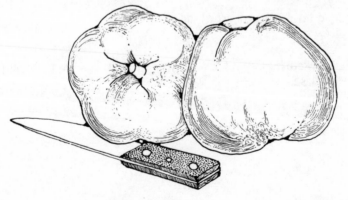

Prune Blancmange

(Serves 3-4)

An interesting way to serve prunes which are a valuable source of roughage and nutrients.

Imperial/Metric
6 prunes, soaked
¼ pint (140ml) unsweetened apple juice
1 teaspoon grated lemon rind
¼ pint (140ml) milk
1 egg, beaten
3 tablespoons brown flaked rice
1 teaspoon lemon juice

American
6 prunes, soaked
⅔ cup unsweetened apple juice
1 teaspoon grated lemon rind
⅔ cup milk
1 egg, beaten
3 tablespoons brown flaked rice
1 teaspoon lemon juice

1. Place prunes, apple juice and lemon rind in a small saucepan and simmer 2-3 minutes until prunes are tender. Discard stones.

2. Whisk milk onto beaten egg, return to saucepan with the flaked rice and stir over a low heat until mixture boils and thickens.

3. Place prunes with juice, sauce and lemon juice in a liquidizer (blender) and run machine until mixture is smooth. Divide between 3 or 4 small pots.

Storage:
In fridge up to 48 hours.

To serve:
Warm or cold with sliced banana and a little natural (plain) yogurt.

Apple and Orange Cup

Any fresh fruit may be liquidized to make a healthy drink. Makes ¾ pint.

Imperial/Metric	**American**
1 large orange	1 large orange
1 dessert apple	1 dessert apple

1. Cut away peel from orange. Roughly chop orange flesh and place in a liquidizer (blender).
2. Wash and roughly chop apple. Add to orange with ¼ pint (140ml/⅔ cup) cold water or sufficient to enable machine to run smoothly and make a smooth purée.
3. Strain immediately and make up to ¾ pint (425ml/2 cups) with cold water.

To serve:
Chilled, with ice cubes or a straw for younger children.

N.B. If your child is already used to orange squash, then you may need to add a few drops of apple concentrate and reduce it gradually thereafter.

Strawberry Shake

For each portion:

Imperial/Metric	**American**
¼ pint (140ml) milk, chilled	⅔ cup milk, chilled
3 or 4 medium-sized strawberries	3 or 4 medium-sized strawberries

1. Wash and hull strawberries and place them in a liquidizer (blender). Add sufficient milk to enable machine to run smoothly to make a purée. Add remaining milk.

To serve:
Pour into a beaker — serve chilled with a slice of strawberry floating on top.

Banana and Yogurt Drink

For each portion:

Imperial/Metric
2 inch (5cm) piece ripe banana
2 fl oz (60ml) natural yogurt
3 fl oz (90ml) milk, chilled

American
2 inch piece ripe banana
¼ cup plain yogurt
⅓ cup milk, chilled

1. Place banana and yogurt in a liquidizer (blender) and run machine until a smooth purée. Add milk.

To serve:
Pour into a beaker and serve chilled with a little grated carob on top.

Fruit Yogurts

Either make your own yogurt using a yogurt maker or buy natural (plain) yogurt — 'live' yogurt contains bacteria beneficial to the digestive system and should be used whenever possible.

Imperial/Metric
¼ pint (140ml) natural yogurt
½ ripe nectarine

American
⅔ cup plain yogurt
½ ripe nectarine

1. Place yogurt with the peeled flesh of the nectarine in a liquidizer and run machine until well blended. Alternatively, finely chop or mash nectarines and stir into yogurt.

Other suitable fruits: banana, strawberries, peach, mango.

3.

TODDLER'S TEA PARTY

Children's parties seem to overflow with an abundance of sugary drinks and party food, rounded off with a 'going home bag' filled with tooth rotting 'goodies'. Nobody would expect you to send your child to a party with his own 'healthy' food tucked under his arm, but if he has never eaten very sugary foods, he'll not enjoy them now and certainly won't overeat.

A wise mother will steer a moderate course when it comes to her turn for party food and the following suggestions show how to make exciting healthy food without spoiling the party fun!

1. Children love 'bits' of food so start with cubes of cheese, small sticks of celery, carrots and cucumber, plain crisps, cheese biscuits or straws, breadsticks, raisins, small nuts (for older children). Homemade popcorn. Remove stones from dates and fill with cheese.

2. Make duet sandwiches using one wholemeal (wheat) slice and one white slice of bread to cater for all tastes. Cut into small fingers or use petit fours cutters.

3. Fill small pastry cases with cottage or cream cheese, scrambled egg or cooked vegetables moistened with natural (plain) yogurt.

4. Only introduce the 'sweeter' foods when the children have filled up on the savouries.

5. Make your own jelly, blancmange and ice cream, or just serve an ice cream scoop in a cone to each child — no one will want to ask for the chocolate sauce!

6. Make small cakes in petit-fours cases and leave the Birthday cake until last.

Drinks
Make up jugs of diluted unsweetened fruit juice and serve with ice cubes and a straw. It has an added bonus of not staining carpets or party clothes if spilt

as the squashes, syrups and fizzy drinks do.

Diddy Bags

Find alternatives for prizes or going-home presents. Balloons, pencils, rubbers, notepads, sticky tape, stickers, badges, whistles, plasticine, small box of raisins, a small orange or banana, or a personalized home-made biscuit are just as acceptable and probably less expensive too!

Teddy Bear Cake

Date Cake

Dates replace the sugar in this recipe and help to keep the cake moist. Best made one day before being used.

Imperial/Metric
½ lb (225g) stoned dates
6 oz (170g) butter, softened
2 eggs, beaten
10 oz (285g) self-raising wholemeal
  flour*
1 teaspoon baking powder
3 tablespoons vegetable oil

American
1½ cups pitted dates
⅔ cup butter, softened
2 eggs, beaten
2½ cups self-raising wholewheat
  flour*
1 teaspoon baking powder
3 tablespoons vegetable oil

1. Cover dates with boiling water and leave to soak overnight. Strain and reserve liquid.

2. Prepare a moderate oven 350°F/180°C (Gas Mark 4). Grease and line a 12×8 inch (30.5×20.5cm) baking or roasting tin.

3. Beat dates until smooth, add butter and cream together. Beat in eggs.

4. Mix flour and baking powder together and fold into dates with vegetable oil and ¼ pint (140ml/⅔ cup) reserved liquid. Leave 2 minutes, adding extra liquid if necessary, to make a soft, dropping consistency.

5. Spread mixture into tin; level top. Bake 40-45 minutes until evenly brown and firm. Cool in tin.

Storage:
When cold wrap in foil 2-3 days or freeze until required.

*N.B. If not available, use wholemeal (wheat) flour with 3 teaspoons extra baking powder.

To assemble cake:

Imperial/Metric
1 cake
Double quantity Carob Spread (see
  (page 66)
2 Shredded Wheat, crushed*
1 oz (30g) Almond Paste (see page
  131)
Desiccated coconut

American
1 cake
Double quantity Carob Spread (see
  (page 66)
2 Shredded Wheat, crushed*
¼ cup Almond Paste (see page 131)
Desiccated coconut

*Note: All-bran, Weetabix or wheatflake cereal may be used.

1. Cover a 15×11 inch (38×28cm) piece of cardboard with foil. Draw a paper pattern of Teddy Bear as illustrated in Figure 1, the same size as the cake, and cut out.

2. Place on cake and cut round with a sharp knife.

3. Place cake on prepared board and stick on feet and paws with a little icing.

4. Cover top and sides of cake with icing (reserve a little for board).

5. Sprinkle Shredded Wheat over cake; press up sides with a knife.

6. Use almond paste to make nose and eyes.

7. Slacken reserved icing with a little milk and spread thinly over foil. Sprinkle coconut over board and press down lightly. Your Teddy Bear is now finished (Figure 2).

Storage:
Keep in a cool place until required. Wrap left over cake in foil and keep in fridge for up to one week.

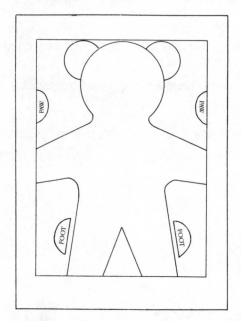

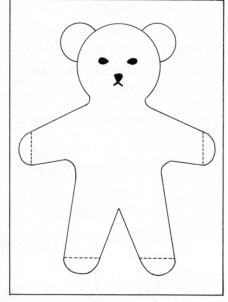

Figure 1: Pattern for Teddy Bear Cake.   **Figure 2:** Finished Teddy Bear Cake.

Pinwheel Sandwiches

Imperial/Metric	**American**
1 uncut wholemeal bread loaf	1 uncut wholewheat bread loaf
Butter	Butter

Fillings:

Cream cheese or sieved cottage cheese	Cream cheese or sieved cottage cheese
Grated cheese moistened with a little natural yogurt	Grated cheese moistened with a little plain yogurt
Nut Butter (see page 88)	Nut Butter (see page 88)
Low-salt vegetable or yeast extract/spread	Low-salt vegetable or yeast extract/spread
Dried dates or apricots, softened and mashed	Dried dates or apricots, softened and mashed
Pear 'n Apple Spread	Pear 'n Apple Spread

1. Remove crusts from loaf and cut thin slices down length of loaf.

2. Spread slices with butter and preferred filling.

3. Tightly roll up each slice down length, wrap individual rolls in wetted greaseproof paper and twist ends like a cracker.

4. Wrap rolls together in a damp tea towel. Keep in fridge until required.

To serve:
Unwrap rolls and cut into ½ inch (1.3cm) thick slices. Cover plate with clingfilm until served.

Cheesy Straws

(Makes 24)

A favourite with all ages, these straws also make an alternative choice for the biscuit tin.

Imperial/Metric	American
4 oz (115g) wholemeal flour	1 cup wholewheat flour
2 teaspoons baking powder	2 teaspoons baking powder
¼ teaspoon dry mustard	¼ teaspoon dry mustard
2 oz (55g) butter	¼ cup butter
2 oz (55g) mature Cheddar cheese, grated	½ cup grated hard cheese
2 tablespoons beaten egg	2 tablespoons beaten egg
1 tablespoon water	1 tablespoon water

Glazing:

Beaten egg	Beaten egg
3 tablespoons sesame seeds	3 tablespoons sesame seeds
or	*or*
1 oz (30g) Cheddar cheese, grated	¼ cup hard grated cheese

1. Prepare a fairly hot oven 400°F/200°C (Gas Mark 6). Flour a large baking sheet.

2. Mix flour, baking powder and mustard together in a bowl. Add butter, cut up, and rub into flour.

3. Stir in grated cheese, egg and sufficient water to make a soft dough. Knead lightly until smooth.

4. Roll out pastry to an oblong 12 × 4 inches (30.5 × 10cm).

5. Brush with beaten egg and sprinkle over the sesame seeds or grated cheese.

6. Cut pastry into ½ inch (1.3cm) wide fingers across width. Place fingers on baking sheet and bake 10-12 minutes until golden brown. Cool slightly then carefully place on cooling tray.

Storage:
In an airtight tin up to 3 days. If not using same day, gently freshen up in a warm oven for a few minutes.

Carob Clusters

(Makes about 16)

Use the small petit-fours cases for these clusters as they have more substance than the traditional Chocolate Krispies.

Imperial/Metric	American
2×2 oz (60g) bars block dessert carob	2×2 ounce bars block dessert carob
1 oz (30g) butter	2 tablespoons butter
3 oz (85g) wheatflakes	1 cup wheatflakes
1 oz (30g) sultanas, roughly chopped	¼ cup golden seedless raisins, roughly chopped
1 tablespoon chopped hazelnuts	1 tablespoon chopped hazelnuts
1 teaspoon finely grated orange rind	1 teaspoon finely grated orange rind

1. Break up carob and place in a bowl with the butter. Melt carob over a bowl of hot water or in a microwave oven.

2. Stir in wheatflakes, sultanas (golden seedless raisins), nuts and orange rind. Mix well until ingredients are evenly coated.

3. Divide mixture between small paper cases and place in fridge for 1 hour until firm.

Variations:
1. Omit nuts and stir in 1 tablespoon desiccated or crushed flaked coconut.

2. Use the orange flavoured carob and omit orange rind.

Ginger Boys

(Makes 8-10)

If you make a hole in these before baking they can be hung up with ribbon during the party. Use a shaped cutter or make a cardboard pattern.

Imperial/Metric	American
½ lb (225g) wholemeal flour	2 cups wholewheat flour
2 teaspoons baking powder	2 teaspoons baking powder
1 teaspoon ground ginger	1 teaspoon ground ginger
6 oz (170g) butter	¾ cup butter
4 tablespoons apple concentrate	4 tablespoons apple concentrate

Decoration:

1 egg yolk, beaten

Currants for eyes

1 egg yolk, beaten

Currants for eyes

1. Prepare a moderately hot oven 375°F/190°C (Gas Mark 5). Flour 2 baking sheets.

2. Mix flour, baking powder and ground ginger together in a bowl. Add butter, cut up, and rub into flour.

3. Add apple concentrate and mix with a fork to make a soft dough. Knead lightly on a floured surface until smooth.

4. Roll dough out to ⅛ inch (.3cm) thickness and cut out shapes. Place on prepared baking sheet. Brush with beaten egg yolk, to glaze. Press in currants for eyes, buttons, etc.

5. Bake 12-15 minutes until firm, brushing half way through cooking with the egg yolk. Cool biscuits on a wire tray.

6. Alternatively, using a 2 inch (5cm) cutter, cut out rounds.

Storage:

Store in an airtight tin or wrapped in foil for 2 to 3 days.

Overleaf: From Toddler's Tea Party section: Fruit in Jelly (page 68), Carob Clusters (page 64), Pinwheel Sandwiches (page 62).

Opposite: From Teenage Party Fayre section: Fruit Cup (page 76), Tomato Sauce (page 72), Jacket Potatoes with Walnut and Avocado Topping (page 72), Swiss Cheese Fondue Sauce (page 73).

Fruity Ice Cream

(Makes about 8 servings)

Use any fruit — raspberries give a good colour, but tend to be a little sharp.

Imperial/Metric	**American**
14 oz (395g) can fruit in natural juice	14 oz (395g) can fruit in natural juice
½ pint (285ml) evaporated milk, chilled	1⅓ cups evaporated milk, chilled

1. Purée fruit with juice (sieve if necessary and discard pips). Pour purée into a shallow dish, cover with foil and place in the freezer or ice cube compartment until frozen about 1 inch (2.5cm) in around edges.

2. Whisk evaporated milk until thick. Beat or whisk purée until slushy, then fold quickly into evaporated milk. Return to freezer, covered, until just beginning to freeze round edges.

3. Turn mixture into a chilled bowl, whisk well and quickly divide between clean yogurt pots, cover and freeze.

To serve:
Place pots in fridge 15-20 minutes before serving.

Carob Spread

This makes sufficient to sandwich and top a 7 inch (18cm) cake.

Imperial/Metric	**American**
4 oz (115g) orange flavoured block carob	2 bars (100g) orange flavored block carob
1 oz (30g) butter	2 tablespoons butter
½ lb (225g) cream cheese	1 cup cream cheese
Milk, to mix	Milk, to mix

1. Break up carob and place in a small bowl with the butter. Melt over hot water or in the microwave oven. Cool.

2. Beat cream cheese until smooth, then beat in carob and sufficient milk to make a soft, fluffy-textured spread. Alternatively use an electric whisk.

Storage:
Cover and keep in the fridge for up to 2-3 days. Not suitable for freezing unless sandwiched inside a cake.

Banana Finger Biscuits

(Makes about 24)

This mixture can be cut into a variety of shapes, but keep them small for even baking.

Imperial/Metric	American
4 oz (115g) wholemeal flour	1 cup wholewheat flour
1 teaspoon baking powder	1 teaspoon baking powder
2 oz (55g) butter, softened	¼ cup butter, softened
1 small, ripe banana	1 small, ripe banana

1. Prepare a moderately hot oven 375°F/190°C (Gas Mark 5). Dust 2 baking sheets with flour.

2. Place flour, baking powder and butter in a bowl. Mash banana, add to bowl and mix with a fork until mixture binds to make a soft dough. Knead lightly on a floured surface.

3. Roll out to the thickness of pastry and prick with a fork. Cut into ¾ inch (2cm) wide strips and into 2½ inch (6.5cm) lengths. Place biscuits on prepared baking sheets and bake just above centre of oven for 15-20 minutes until evenly golden. Cool on wire tray.

Storage:
In an airtight tin 3-4 days.

To serve:
On their own or with ends dipped in melted carob.

Fruit in Jelly

(Serves 10)

Use a mixture of unsweetened fruit juices for the best flavour, e.g., orange and apple juice. This 'jelly' sets ready to eat within half-an-hour.

Imperial/Metric	American
1 dessert apple	1 dessert apple
1 orange	1 orange
1 pear	1 pear
10 grapes	10 grapes
2 pints (1 litre) unsweetened fruit juices	2 pints unsweetened fruit juices
4 teaspoons vegetable gel	4 teaspoons vegetable gel

1. Prepare fruit and cut into small cubes. Mix together, cover and leave 1 hour. Drain and divide between ten small dishes.

2. Place 1 pint (570ml/2½ cups) fruit juice in a small saucepan, warm gently but do not boil. Sprinkle over vegetable gel and whisk until dissolved. Remove from heat and stir in remaining juices.

3. Pour liquid immediately over fruit (about 4 fl oz/115ml/⅓ cup per serving). Leave to set.

To serve:
On its own or with ice cream.

N.B. Alternatively use a 14 oz (395g/2 cups) can mixed fruit salad and make juice up to required amount.

4.

TEENAGER'S PARTY FAYRE

Teenagers are in the high risk group because of their vast consumption of soft drinks and fast food. But healthy foods can be fun too, and with a little imagination can appeal to even the faddiest teenager.

Drinks

All canned and bottled drinks contain a high proportion of sugar and 'low-calorie' drinks are sweetened with 'artificial' sweeteners. The wide range of unsweetened fruit juices available can form the base of non-alcoholic punches. Liven them up with soda, tonic or sparkling mineral waters, ice cubes, fresh fruit, and herbs. Serve with elaborate straws.

Ice-cold milk shakes are fun to make — just leave a selection of soft fruit and chilled milk by the blender and let them make their own.

Savouries

These are much nicer if served warm. Make a selection of pizzas and quiches and pop into a moderate oven just as the guests arrive. Jacket potatoes with a selection of 'help yourself' fillings are popular, but do provide plastic, rather than paper, plates.

Nibbles go down well with any age group so provide plenty of plain crisps, bread sticks, nuts, dried fruit, cubes of cheese, cheese straws, savoury crackers, crispbread, home-popped corn, poppadoms, sticks of celery, carrot, cucumber, red or green pepper and radishes. The vegetables can be kept fresh by standing them in a little cold water.

Dips made with cream cheese, natural (plain) yogurt, sieved cottage cheese or puréed vegetables are popular, too. And don't forget the cheeseboard with fresh wholemeal (wheat) French sticks or bread to go with it.

The Cake

Many teenagers may prefer not to have a birthday cake, but chocolate cakes are always popular. Use carob flour instead of cocoa and it is very unlikely they'll spot the difference.

Ice cream seems to be the all-time favourite with any age group, but don't serve with a thick syrupy sauce.

Finally:
If you can't seat all the guests clear a room of furniture and cover the carpet from wall to wall with a heavy-weight piece of plastic. Scatter plenty of cushions over the floor. After supper, the plastic can be rolled up for the dancing, and don't forget a few low-wattage lamps for atmosphere.

Savoury Burgers

(Makes 20)

These delicious burgers make an excellent family lunch or supper dish, so make some extra for the freezer.

Imperial/Metric	American
4 oz (115g) Country Soup Mixture (beans, barley, peas, rice, lentils)	½ cup Country Soup Mixture (beans, barley, peas, rice, lentils)
1 oz (30g) red lentils	2½ tablespoons red lentils
1×14 oz (395g) tin tomatoes in juice	2⅓ cups canned tomatoes in juice
1 large onion, finely chopped	1 large onion, finely chopped
3 sticks celery, finely chopped	3 stalks celery, finely chopped
1 lb (455g) potatoes, peeled and finely chopped	2½ cups peeled and finely chopped potatoes
2 oz (55g) chopped walnuts	½ cup chopped English walnuts
1 teaspoon curry powder	1 teaspoon curry powder
2 teaspoons soya sauce	2 teaspoons soy sauce
¼ teaspoon chilli powder	¼ teaspoon chili powder
2 teaspoons low-salt vegetable or yeast extract/spread	2 teaspoons low-salt vegetable or yeast extract/spread
2 tablespoons freshly chopped parsley	2 tablespoons freshly chopped parsley
2 oz (55g) rolled oats	½ cup rolled oats
½ lb (225g) fresh wholemeal breadcrumbs	4 cups wholewheat breadcrumbs
1 egg, beaten	1 egg, beaten
Vegetable oil	Vegetable oil

1. Soak Country Soup mixture and lentils in cold water overnight. Rinse well and place in a large heavy-based pan with 1 pint (570ml/2½ cups) water. Bring to boil and boil for 10 minutes.

2. Add tomatoes and juice, onion, celery, potatoes, walnuts, curry powder, soy(a) sauce, chilli powder, yeast or vegetable extract and parsley. Return to the boil, cover and reduce heat. Simmer over a very low heat for 2 hours, stirring occasionally, until all ingredients are soft and mixture is thick. Cool mixture and place in fridge for several hours or overnight.

3. Stir in rolled oats and 3 oz (85g/1½ cups) breadcrumbs or sufficient to make a thick paste.

4. Using a tablespoon, place heaped spoons of mixture onto a clean surface and lightly shape into burgers with wetted hands. Place on a tray covered with foil and chill.

5. Brush burgers with beaten egg then coat in remaining breadcrumbs. Fry in vegetable oil 2-3 minutes each side until golden brown and heated through.

Storage:
Freeze burgers after coating with breadcrumbs or fry 1 minute each side, cool rapidly and open freeze. Store up to 1 month. Thaw in fridge and heat through in oven or under grill.

To serve:
Serve in warmed wholemeal (wholewheat) baps with cooked onions, Tomato Sauce (see page 72) or grated (hard) cheese.

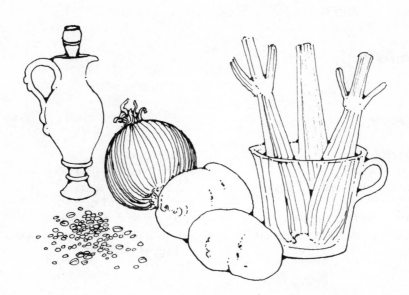

Tomato Sauce

(Makes about 1 lb/445g)

Imperial/Metric
1 large onion, finely chopped
1 clove garlic, crushed
2 × 14 oz (395g) tin tomatoes in juice
2 oz (55g) raisins
Pinch each of: chilli powder, dry
    mustard, ground ginger, ground
    cinnamon
4 teaspoons cider or wine vinegar

American
1 large onion, finely chopped
1 clove garlic, minced
4 cups tomatoes in juice
⅓ cup raisins
Pinch each of: chili powder, dry
    mustard, ground ginger, ground
    cinnamon
4 teaspoons cider or wine vinegar

1. Place onion, garlic, tomatoes and juice in a saucepan. Add raisins, chilli powder, mustard, ginger and cinnamon.

2. Bring slowly to boil then simmer gently for 15 minutes or until mixture is reduced to a pulp.

3. Rub mixture through a sieve (strainer) and discard pips. Return mixture to pan and add vinegar. Re-boil then simmer 2-3 minutes. Place in hot sterilized jars and seal.

Storage:
Up to 1 week in the fridge or freeze in small quantities.

Potato Topping 1

Avocado and Walnut

(Makes 7 fl oz/200ml/¾ cup)

Imperial/Metric
1 ripe avocado pear
¼ pint (140ml) natural yogurt
Freshly ground pepper
6 drops Tabasco Sauce
2 tablespoons finely chopped
    walnuts
Paprika

American
1 ripe avocado pear
⅔ cup plain yogurt
Freshly ground pepper
6 drops Tabasco Sauce
2 tablespoons finely chopped
    English walnuts
Paprika

1. Halve, discard stone and scoop out avocado flesh and place in a liquidizer (blender). Add yogurt, pepper and Tabasco Sauce and run machine until smooth.

2. Stir in walnuts, adjust seasoning, and place in a serving bowl. Cover tightly with cling film and chill for one hour.

Storage:
Covered in fridge 6-8 hours, but discolouration will occur: stir before serving.

To serve:
Gently stir mixture and sprinkle top with paprika.

Potato Topping 2

Fondue Sauce

(Makes about ¾ pint/425ml/2 cups)

This sauce can be served hot with baked potatoes or cold as a dip — Cheddar cheese gives a softer, more manageable texture than the traditional 'stringy' cheeses usually used for fondue.

Imperial/Metric	American
7 fl oz (200ml) unsweetened apple juice	¾ cup unsweetened apple juice
10 oz (285g) mature Cheddar cheese, grated	2½ cups mature hard cheese, grated
½ teaspoon dry mustard	½ teaspoon dry mustard
4 teaspoons arrowroot	4 teaspoons arrowroot

1. Heat apple juice in a saucepan over a moderate heat. Gradually stir in cheese until dissolved.

2. Blend mustard and arrowroot with a little water, pour into cheese mixture and continue stirring until mixture just begins to bubble and thickly coats back of spoon. Do not overcook.

3. Pour into a serving bowl, cover and keep warm.

To serve:
Serve hot as soon after making as possible, or serve cold, stirring and slackening with a little milk, if necessary to make a dip. Do not freeze.

Mock Chocolate Sauce

(Makes about ½ pint/285ml/1⅓ cups)

This can be served cold on ice cream or as a hot sauce on puddings.

Imperial/Metric	American
4 oz (115g) stoned dates	¾ cup pitted dates
2 tablespoons carob powder	2 tablespoons carob powder
2 tablespoons hot water	2 tablespoons hot water
4 oz (115g) cream cheese	8 tablespoons cream cheese

1. Cover dates with cold water and leave overnight.

2. Blend carob powder and water together until smooth.

3. Drain dates and reserve juice. Place dates in a liquidizer (blender) with the carob and cream cheese. Run machine and add sufficient date juice to make a smooth, coating sauce.

Storage:
In fridge 2-3 days or freeze. Thaw in fridge and beat well before using.

To serve:
Use cold, or heat gently without boiling.

Apple Ice Cream

(Makes about 2 pints/1 litre/5 cups)

Imperial/Metric	American
1 lb (455g) cooking apples, cored and chopped	2 cups chopped, cored cooking apples
Knob of butter	Knob of butter
Unsweetened apple juice	Unsweetened apple juice
¼ pint (140ml) double cream	⅔ cup heavy cream
¼ pint (140ml) evaporated milk, chilled	⅔ cup evaporated milk, chilled
1 egg white	1 egg white

1. Place apple, butter, 3 tablespoons apple juice and 3 tablespoons water in a pan. Cover and cook over a low heat until soft.

2. Purée apples and make up to 1 pint (570ml/2 ½ cups) with apple juice. Pour into a shallow dish and cover with foil. Place in the freezer or ice cube making compartment until just beginning to freeze round edge.

3. Whisk cream, evaporated milk, and egg white separately until thick.

4. Beat apple purée until slushy. Carefully fold in cream, evaporated milk and egg white. Cover and return to freezer until just beginning to freeze round edge.

5. Beat hard, cover with foil and return to freezer until firm.

Storage:
Up to 1 month.

To serve:
Place in fridge 40-50 minutes before serving.

Knickerbocker Glories

An old-time favourite with a healthier taste.

Imperial/Metric
Fresh fruit or tinned fruit in natural
  juice
Banana
Apple Ice Cream (see page 74)
Mock Chocolate Sauce (see page
  74)
Flaked or chopped nuts, toasted

American
Fresh fruit or canned fruit in natural
  juice
Banana
Apple Ice Cream (see page 74)
Mock Chocolate Sauce (see page
  74)
Flaked or chopped nuts, toasted

1. Prepare fruit and slice. Layer with spoons of ice cream into tall sundae glasses.

2. Drizzle about 1 tablespoon sauce over each.

3. Sprinkle with nuts.

Variations:
Different flavoured ice creams may be used see Banana Ice Cream (page 47) or Fruity Ice Cream (page 66).

Fruit Cup

(Makes about 2½ pints/1½ litres plus soda)

A special tea, e.g. Earl Grey, gives a pleasant flavour.

Imperial/Metric
½ pint (285ml) freshly made tea,
   chilled
1 pint (570ml) unsweetened apple
   juice
2 large oranges, sliced
1 large lemon, sliced
1 pint (570ml) unsweetened, non-
   alcoholic red grape juice, chilled
Soda water

American
1⅓ cup freshly made tea, chilled
2½ cups unsweetened apple juice
2 large oranges, sliced
1 large lemon, sliced
2½ cups unsweetened, non-
   alcoholic red grape juice, chilled
Soda water

1. Place tea, apple juice, orange and lemon slices in a large bowl. Leave in a
    cool place several hours or overnight.

2. Add chilled grape juice.

To serve:
Pour into individual glasses and top up with soda water. Add ice cubes, a slice
of fruit and a straw.

Apricot Spread

This versatile spread can be used instead of butter icing or spread thinly as a
sandwich filler.

Imperial/Metric
8 apricot halves tinned in natural
   juice, drained
6 oz (170g) cream cheese
Few drops lemon juice

American
8 apricot halves canned in natural
   juice, drained
⅔ cup cream cheese
Few drops lemon juice

1. Purée or sieve the apricots. Beat the cheese and lemon juice until smooth,
    then gradually beat in puréed apricots (alternatively place apricots and cheese
    in a blender or food processor and run machine until mixture is light and
    creamy). Chill before use.

Variation:
Stir in finely chopped toasted nuts.

Nut Drops

(Makes about 24)

A delicate biscuit (cookie) to serve with desserts and ice cream.

Imperial/Metric	**American**
2 oz (55g) shelled hazelnuts, toasted	½ cup shelled hazelnuts, toasted
2 oz (55g) butter	¼ cup butter
1 tablespoon apple concentrate	1 tablespoon apple concentrate
1½ oz (45g) wholemeal flour	5 tablespoons wholewheat flour
2 egg whites	2 egg whites

1. Prepare a fairly hot oven 400°F/200°C (Gas Mark 6). Oil a baking sheet or cover with baking parchment.

2. Chop hazelnuts. Melt butter and stir in hazelnuts, apple concentrate and flour.

3. Whisk egg whites until stiff. Carefully fold into mixture until well blended.

4. Using a teaspoon, place two level spoons of mixture for each biscuit on the tray, leaving a little room between each.

5. Bake 7-8 minutes until golden brown on edges. Remove immediately with a spatula and leave to cool and crispen slightly on a cooking tray. Repeat with remaining mixture.

Storage:
These tend to soften if stored in an airtight tin. Eat within 2-3 days.

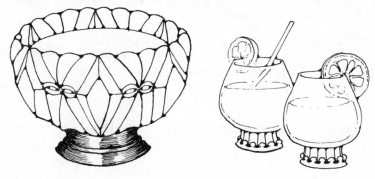

Orange Cheesecake

(Serves 8-10)

This quick, no-cook base can be used for a variety of cold desserts.

Imperial/Metric   **American**

Base:

3 oz (85g) butter   ⅓ cup butter
2 oz (55g) chopped nuts, toasted   ½ cup chopped nuts, toasted
3 oz (85g) wheatflakes, toasted   1¾ cups wheatflakes, toasted
½ teaspoon ground ginger   ½ teaspoon ground ginger

Topping:

Rind and juice of 2 large oranges   Rind and juice of 2 large oranges
6 oz (170g) cream cheese   ⅔ cup cream cheese
1 egg, separated   1 egg, separated
¼ pint (140ml) single cream   ⅔ cup light cream
2 teaspoons vegetable gel   2 teaspoons vegetable gel

Decoration:

Toasted nuts or wheatflakes   Toasted nuts or wheatflakes

1. *Base:* Grease an 8 inch (20.5cm) loose-bottomed tin. Melt butter, stir in nuts, wheatflakes and ground ginger. Press mixture firmly onto base of tin. Chill.

2. *Filling:* Place orange rind and cheese in a bowl and beat until smooth. Add egg yolk and when well mixed, gradually beat in cream. Whisk egg white until stiff and reserve to one side.

3. Make orange juice up to ½ pint with water, if necessary. Bring just to boiling point, remove from heat and whisk in vegetable gel until dissolved. (Alternatively, follow method on packet). Continue whisking until juice begins to thicken. Add all at once to cheese mixture, whisking continuously until well mixed.

4. Fold in egg whites and pour mixture over prepared base. Chill 1 hour or until firm.

N.B. Mixture may tend to be 'lumpy' if vegetable gel sets too quickly. Re-heat gel gently until melted or liquidize or sieve (strain) mixture, if already added to cheese.

Storage:
2 days in fridge or freeze up to 4 weeks.

To serve:
Remove from tin and sprinkle liberally with nuts or wheatflakes.

Nectar Shake

(2 servings — ¾ pint/425ml/2 cups)

This makes a delicious thick drink that is similar to the milk shakes teenagers love, yet contains no added sugar.

Imperial/Metric	**American**
1 nectarine	1 nectarine
4 strawberries	4 strawberries
¼ pint (140ml) milk, chilled	⅔ cup milk, chilled
¼ pint (140ml) natural yogurt, chilled	⅔ cup plain yogurt, chilled

1. Halve nectarine, discard stone and chop flesh. Hull and halve strawberries.
2. Place strawberries and nectarine in a liquidizer (blender) and run machine until a thick purée. Add milk and yogurt and blend well.

To serve:
Chilled with slices of strawberries.

Variation:
Instead of milk and yogurt, dilute purée with chilled sparkling mineral water, tonic or soda water. Serve chilled.

Dark Apricot Gâteau 1

A moist cake that is best made one day in advance. This cake will not rise as much as a conventional recipe.

Imperial/Metric
3 oz (85g) dried apricots, soaked
2 oz (55g) raisins, soaked
6 oz (170g) soft margarine
3 eggs
6 oz (170g) wholemeal flour
3 teaspoons baking powder
2 tablespoons carob powder

American
⅔ cup dried apricots, soaked
⅓ cup raisins, soaked
⅔ cup soft margarine
3 eggs
1½ cups wholewheat flour
3 teaspoons baking powder
2 tablespoons carob powder

1. Prepare a moderate oven 350°F/180°C (Gas Mark 4). Grease and line base of an 8 inch (20.5cm) tin.

2. Drain apricots and raisins and reserve juice. Liquidize fruit using 2 or 3 tablespoons juice to make machine run smoothly.

3. Place fruit purée and margarine in a bowl and beat together until light and fluffy. Gradually beat in eggs. Mix flour, baking powder and carob powder together, and carefully fold into mixture to make a soft, dropping consistency.

4. Spread mixture into prepared tin and bake for 40-45 minutes until firm. Turn out and cool on a wire tray.

Storage:
When cold wrap in foil and keep up to 4 or 5 days in a cool place.

Dark Apricot Gâteau 2

To assemble cake:

Imperial/Metric
1×Dark Apricot Gâteau (see
  previous recipe)
Double quantity Apricot Spread (see
  page 76)
2 blocks (120g) carob, finely grated
2 oz (55g) finely chopped nuts,
  toasted

American
1×Dark Apricot Gâteau (see
  previous recipe)
Double quantity Apricot Spread (see
  page 76)
2 blocks carob, finely grated
½ cup finely chopped nuts, toasted

1. Split cake through thickness into three layers. Using two-thirds of the icing, sandwich layers together.

2. Spread half the remaining icing round side of cake and roll in grated carob, to coat.

3. Spread remaining icing over top of cake. Mark into 8 or 10 sections and using the nuts and remaining carob, cover the sections alternately. Make a ring of nuts round outer edge, to neaten.

4. Place cake in fridge until required.

Storage:
In fridge up to 24 hours or freeze up to 4 weeks. Thaw slowly in the fridge.

5.

PACKED LUNCHES

Whether by choice or through necessity, the number of children and adults relying on a packed lunch is steadily increasing. The decline of the school canteen service has presented many parents, who don't want their children to eat chips and fizzy drinks at lunch time, with the task of providing an alternative.

However, with a little forward planning, it is possible to pack a healthy, well-balanced meal with the minimum expense and fuss.

The Container
It's worth buying a sturdy plastic lunch box with a handle which seems to have replaced the school satchel in popularity. Most boxes have a non-breakable flask ideal for hot soup or cold drinks. Older children and adults will find a shallow plastic box with a good fitting lid will fit more neatly into brief-cases and bags.

The Food
1. Wholemeal(wheat) baps and pitta bread make a change from bread, the latter making a good envelope for exciting fillings.

2. Small portions of different foods are more enjoyable than a pile of doorstep sandwiches. Use small unbreakable containers for nuts, raisins, home-popped corn, sunflower seeds, etc.

3. Always include a little raw vegetable or fruit. Cos, Webb, or Chinese leaves stay crisp especially if cut into wedges rather than separated into leaves.

4. 'Snack Pots' are suitable for older children and adults. Cook extra rice, pasta, or potatoes and add 'bits' of whatever you have in the fridge, such as cheese, cooked vegetables and beans and raw vegetables. Moisten with left-over gravy, sauces, milk or yogurt. Place in a suitable container and don't forget a fork or spoon.

5. Wedge-shaped slices are difficult to carry so make individual pies and pizzas,

or make a large square one, cut up and freeze individual portions. Likewise with cakes, scones, etc. Remove from freezer in the morning.

6. Make 'set' desserts and freeze in yogurt pots. Natural (plain) yogurt makes an excellent dessert — serve with a few raisins or chopped nuts to be stirred in once the pot is opened.

7. For younger children, peel and segment oranges, quarter apple or pear, de-seed grapes. Place them immediately in a clean yogurt pot and cover. Bananas are easy to eat and travel well if not over ripe. Place soft fruit such as halved kiwi fruit, strawberries, and raspberries in a pot too, and provide a spoon and serviette.

Drinks

Fill flask with hot or chilled soup depending on weather. Don't include canned drinks but use unsweetened fruit juices well-diluted, or fill flask with milk. Alternatively just provide a plastic cup for water. For adults, fill flask with boiling water and provide tea, coffee and milk separately.

Finally:
1. Don't include sweets — a small piece of hard cheese eaten at the end of the meal will help to protect the teeth if brushing is not possible.

2. Discourage children from 'swapping' food. They may end up with a white jam sandwich in return for a wholemeal(wheat) cheese one!

Chilled Soup

(Makes 1½ pints/850ml/3¾ cups)

A refreshing uncooked chilled soup that is quickly made in the liquidizer.

Imperial/Metric	**American**
4 oz (115g) cooked haricot beans	⅔ cup cooked navy beans
2 oz (55g) carrot, grated	⅓ cup carrot, grated
3 sticks celery, chopped	3 stalks celery, chopped
3-4 spring onions, chopped	3-4 scallions, chopped
4 tomatoes, chopped	4 tomatoes, chopped
2 tablespoons chopped mint	2 tablespoons chopped mint
Large pinch of chilli powder	Large pinch of chili powder
4 teaspoons tomato purée	4 teaspoons tomato paste
Freshly ground pepper	Freshly ground pepper
Sea salt	Sea salt
½ pint (285ml) water or vegetable water	1⅓ cups water or vegetable water

1. Place beans, carrots, celery, onions, tomatoes, mint, chilli, tomato purée (paste) and a little pepper and salt in a liquidizer (blender). Add half the liquid and run machine until vegetables are smooth. Add remaining liquid.

2. Chill soup in fridge overnight to allow flavours to develop. Adjust seasoning, if necessary.

Storage:
In fridge 2 days or freeze in individual portions. Allow to partly thaw before pouring into chilled flask.

To serve:
Chill flask before filling with chilled soup.

N.B. For extra flavour, add a small crushed clove of garlic.

Pizza Quiches

(Makes 4 individual pizzas)

Imperial/Metric	**American**

Base:

½ lb (225g) wholemeal flour	2 cups wholewheat flour
2 teaspoons baking powder	2 teaspoons baking powder
4 oz (115g) butter or margarine, cut up	½ cup (1 stick) butter or margarine, cut up
Milk, to mix	Milk, to mix

Topping:

14 oz (395g) tin chopped tomatoes in juice	2 cups canned chopped tomatoes in juice
1 teaspoon mixed dried herbs	1 teaspoon mixed dried herbs
7 oz (200g) tin baked beans	1 cup canned beans in tomato sauce
4 oz (115g) Cheddar cheese, grated	1 cup hard grated cheese

1. Prepare a fairly hot oven 400°F/200°C (Gas Mark 6). Grease two baking sheets.

2. *Base:* Mix flour and baking powder together, add butter (margarine) and rub into flour. Add sufficient milk to bind mixture to a soft dough. Knead lightly on a floured surface, until smooth then divide into four, and roll each piece into a 6 inch (15.5cm) circle. Place on prepared trays and pinch up edges.

3. *Topping:* Place tomatoes and herbs in a pan; simmer until reduced to a pulp. Stir in baked beans.

4. Divide mixture between pizza bases. Bake 15 minutes. Sprinkle cheese over pizzas and cook a further 5-10 minutes until cheese has melted and base is cooked. Leave to cool on the trays.

Storage:
When cold wrap in clingfilm or foil. Keep in fridge 2-3 days or freeze.

Variation:

Pasty Pizzas

Place the tomato mixture and cheese onto half the base, dampen the edges and fold over to enclose filling. Seal edges well. Bake as for pizza for 20-25 minutes.

Sandwich Fillers

Wholemeal(wheat) pitta bread makes a change from slices of bread and can hold a lot more filling, too.

To open pitta bread:
Gently warm bread in the oven, microwave oven or under grill. Slice off a thin strip along top of one long side and gently ease bread open. Alternatively cut bread in half across width and open. Allow bread to cool before filling.

Apart from cheese and egg fillings, try some of the following:

Cooked Vegetables
Any left-over vegetables can be finely chopped and moistened with a little natural (plain) yogurt, cottage (pot) or low-fat cream cheese. Parsnips and carrots are sweet when cooked and could be mixed with a few raisins as a dessert.

Dried Fruit
Use apricots, peaches, pears, figs, dates or bananas. Cover with water, bring to boil then leave to cool or soak overnight. Drain, mash and stir in low-fat cream cheese, sieved cottage (pot) cheese, a little natural (plain) yogurt or curd (Ricotta) cheese.

Fresh Fruit
Sliced banana, grated apple, or chopped orange flesh can be mixed with grated (hard) cheese, curd (Ricotta) cheese or peanut butter.

Savoury Caraway Slice

(Makes 8-10 slices)

This pie can be made with any left-over cooked vegetables or beans and the 'scone' — textured pastry crust ensures it travels well.

Imperial/Metric	**American**

Scone Crust:

Imperial/Metric	American
10 oz (285g) wholemeal flour	2½ cups wholewheat flour
4 teaspoons baking powder	4 teaspoons baking powder
4 oz (115g) butter, cut up	½ cup (1 stick) butter, cut up
½ teaspoon caraway seeds	½ teaspoon caraway seeds
Approx. 8 fl oz (240ml) milk	Approx. 1 cup milk

Filling:

1 medium sized onion, sliced	1 medium sized onion, sliced
2 tablespoons vegetable oil	2 tablespoons vegetable oil
6 oz (170g) cooked spinach, well drained and chopped	1 cup cooked spinach, well drained and chopped
4 oz (115g) cooked haricot beans	⅔ cup cooked navy beans
2 oz (55g) mature Cheddar cheese, grated	½ cup mature hard cheese, grated
2 eggs, beaten	2 eggs, beaten
8 fl oz (240ml) milk	1 cup milk
1 teaspoon dried mixed herbs	1 teaspoon dried mixed herbs
Freshly ground pepper	Freshly milled pepper

1. Prepare a moderately hot oven 375°F/190°C (Gas Mark 5). Grease an 8 inch (20.5cm) square tin that is at least 1½ inches (4cm) deep.

2. *Scone Crust:* Place flour and baking powder in a bowl, add butter and rub in. Stir in caraway seeds. Using a fork, add sufficient milk to make a soft dough. Leave 2 minutes then knead lightly on a floured surface until smooth. Use two-thirds to line base and sides of tin.

3. *Filling:* Fry onions in oil until soft, then place in a basin with spinach, beans and cheese and mix lightly together. Lightly whisk eggs, milk, herbs, and a little pepper together and stir into vegetables. Pour mixture into prepared tin. Cover with remaining pastry, sealing edges well. Brush with milk to glaze, and make a hole in the centre.

4. Bake 40-45 minutes until golden and firm in centre. Cool in tin, then cut into slices.

Storage:
In fridge 2 days or wrapped in individual slices in the freezer up to 2 months. This pie may also be eaten while still warm with a salad.

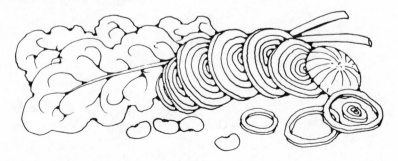

Nut Butter

If you have difficulty finding salt and sugar-free peanut butter, it's quite easy to make your own with an efficient blender.

Imperial/Metric
½ lb (225g) shelled peanuts
2 fl oz (60ml) vegetable oil

American
2 cups shelled peanuts
¼ cup vegetable oil

1. Prepare a moderate oven 350°F/180°C (Gas Mark 4) and spread the nuts out in a baking tin.

2. Roast the nuts, shaking the tin occasionally for ½ hour or until nuts are golden brown. Leave to cool.

3. Place nuts in a blender and run machine until finely ground. With the machine still going, gradually add sufficient oil to make a soft spreadable consistency.

Storage:
In a screw-top jar in the fridge. Use as a sandwich filler mixed with savoury vegetables or fruit.

Variation:
Use cashew nuts or a mixture of nuts.

Rock Buns

(Makes 12)

Imperial/Metric
½ lb (225g) wholemeal flour
2 teaspoons baking powder
4 oz (115g) margarine or butter, cut
  up
1 teaspoon mixed spice
3 oz (85g) stoned dates, finely
  chopped
2 oz (55g) currants
1 egg, beaten
Milk

American
2 cups wholewheat flour
2 teaspoons baking powder
1 stick (½ cup) margarine or butter,
  cut up
1 teaspoon mixed spice
½ cup finely chopped dates
⅓ cup currants
1 egg, beaten
Milk

1. Prepare a hot oven 425°F/220°C (Gas Mark 7). Grease two baking sheets.

2. Mix flour and baking powder together, add fat and rub into flour. Stir in spice, dates and currants.

3. Reserve a little egg to glaze. Add remainder with sufficient milk to bind ingredients to a stiff dough.

4. Place mixture in 'rocky' piles on prepared baking sheets. Brush the buns all over with reserved egg.

5. Bake 10 minutes, reduce heat to 375°F/190°C (Gas Mark 5) for a further 5-10 minutes until buns are golden brown. Do not overcook. Cool on a wire tray.

Storage:
When cold, store up to 4 days in an airtight tin or wrapped in foil.

Choconut Bites

(Makes 49×1 inch (2.5cm) squares)

These are similar to Health Bars, but contain no honey or brown sugar as many of the commercial varieties do.

Imperial/Metric
2 oz (55g) hazelnuts, toasted and
    chopped
1 oz (30g) sesame seeds
3 oz (85g) sultanas, chopped
4 oz (115g) porridge oats
3 tablespoons carob powder
6 tablespoons vegetable oil
1 large egg
2 tablespoons Pear 'n Apple spread

American
½ cup hazelnuts, toasted and
    chopped
¼ cup sesame seeds
½ cup golden seedless raisins,
    chopped
1 cup rolled oats
3 tablespoons carob powder
6 tablespoons vegetable oil
1 large egg
2 tablespoons Pear 'n Apple spread

1. Prepare a moderate oven 350°F/180°C (Gas Mark 4). Line the base of a 7 inch (18cm) square tin with foil.

2. Place nuts, sesame seeds, sultanas (golden seedless raisins) oats, carob powder, oil, egg and Pear 'n Apple spread in a bowl and mix well to bind together.

3. Press mixture firmly into tin.

4. Bake 20 minutes. Cool in tin then cut into small squares. When cold, lift out foil and carefully remove squares.

Storage:
In an airtight tin for up to 1 week.

N.B. Malt extract may be used instead of Pear 'n Apple spread, but they will be sweeter.

Figgy Rolls

(Makes about 16)

These rolls can also be served warm with custard sauce or yogurt as a dessert.

Imperial/Metric	American
6 oz (170g) dried figs, soaked	1¼ cups dried figs, soaked
6 oz (170g) wholemeal flour	1½ cups wholewheat flour
2 teaspoons baking powder	2 teaspoons baking powder
1 teaspoon ground cinnamon	1 teaspoon ground cinnamon
4 oz (115g) butter, softened	1 stick (½ cup) butter, softened
1 large egg, beaten	1 large egg, beaten
1 small dessert apple	1 small dessert apple

1. Prepare a moderate oven 350°F/180°C (Gas Mark 4). Lightly flour a large baking sheet.

2. Drain and purée figs.

3. Place flour, baking powder, cinnamon and butter in a bowl. Reserve a little egg for glazing and add remainder to bowl. Mix with a fork to bind ingredients together. Knead lightly on a floured surface.

4. Roll out dough to 12 × 8 inch (30.5 × 20.5cm). Cut into two equal strips down length.

5. Wash and grate apple into figs and mix lightly together.

6. Place fig mixture down centre of each strip. Dampen edges and roll strips up loosely with joins underneath. Cut each roll in half with a diagonal cut and place the four rolls on the prepared baking sheet. Make 3 short cuts diagonally across each roll. Glaze with reserved egg.

7. Bake 25-30 minutes until firm and golden brown. Leave 5 minutes then carefully transfer to a cooling tray. When cold, cut into pieces.

Storage:
Wrap in foil and keep in fridge 2-3 days or freeze individually wrapped slices for packed lunches.

Orangechoc Pudding

(Makes 4-5 servings)

Use block carob instead of powder for a rich-flavoured dessert.

Imperial/Metric	**American**
¾ pint (425ml) milk	2 cups milk
Grated rind and juice of 1 orange	Grated rind and juice of 1 orange
2 oz (55g) wholemeal semolina	½ cup wholewheat semolina
¼ pint (140ml) evaporated milk	⅔ cup evaporated milk
½ bar (30g) block carob, chopped	½ bar (30g) block carob, chopped

1. Place milk, orange rind and semolina in a small pan. Bring slowly to the boil, reduce heat and simmer, stirring occasionally, until mixture is thick. Discard rind.

2. Gradually stir in evaporated milk and stir over a low heat until mixture thickly coats back of spoon. Remove from heat and stir in carob. Cool, stirring occasionally.

3. Beat in 4-6 teaspoons orange juice, to slacken, then divide mixture between empty yogurt pots, cover and chill.

Storage:
In fridge 2 days or frozen up to 4 weeks.

To serve:
Stir in a few raisins or chopped nuts.

N.B. Do not boil mixture once evaporated milk has been added as it burns easily.

Cheese 'n' Apple Turnovers

(Makes 10)

Use cooked apple to ensure the filling doesn't shrink and leave hollow spaces. Use a tasty, crumbly cheese.

Imperial/Metric	American

Filling:

½ lb (225g) prepared cooking apples, sliced	1⅓ cup prepared, sliced cooking apples
¼ teaspoon ground nutmeg	¼ teaspoon ground nutmeg
4 tablespoons unsweetened apple or orange juice	4 tablespoons unsweetened apple or orange juice
5 oz (140g) Caerphilly or Wensleydale cheese, crumbled	1¼ cups hard cheese, crumbled

Pastry:

½ lb (225g) wholemeal flour	2 cups wholewheat flour
4 oz (115g) butter, cut up	½ cup (1 stick) butter, cut up
1 small egg, beaten	1 small egg, beaten
Milk, to mix	Milk, to mix
2 tablespoons sesame seeds	2 tablespoons sesame seeds

1. Prepare a fairly hot oven 400°F/200°C (Gas Mark 6). Flour two baking sheets.

2. *Filling:* Place apple, nutmeg and fruit juice in a small pan, cover with a well-fitting lid and cook over a low heat until apples are just soft but still hold their shape. Cool.

3. *Pastry:* Place flour in a bowl. Add butter and rub in. Make egg up to 6 fl oz (180ml/scant ¾ cup) with milk and mix sufficient in to flour to make a soft dough. Knead lightly on a floured surface until smooth then cut pastry into ten equal pieces. Sprinkle sesame seeds over work surface and roll each piece of pastry into a 4 inch (10cm) circle.

4. Divide apple and cheese between circles. Dampen edges, fold over pastry and seal edges well. Place on prepared baking sheets. Brush with fruit juice, or egg and milk to glaze.

5. Bake 15-20 minutes until golden brown.

Storage:
In fridge 24 hours or freeze for up to 2 months.

N.B. These turnovers may also be eaten warm with custard as a pudding.

6.

FAMILY CAKES

Afternoon tea with delicate sandwiches and fancy cakes is an event of the past for many, but cakes, especially the rich, sugary gâteaux, seem to be as popular as ever. Even the 'plainer' cakes contain a high percentage of sugar so it is wise and cheaper to make your own.

Sugar in Cookery

Sugar not only sweetens a recipe, but has the following qualities:

1. Helps the fat to whisk up and hold air.

2. Prolongs the keeping quality of the cake.

3. Helps to soften the gluten in the flour and produce a soft textured cake.

When heated, the sugar melts and combines with the liquid in the cake mixture to form a syrup. The thicker the syrup, the softer the cake texture.

Reducing the Sugar

It is possible to reduce the quantity of sugar in a recipe by up to 50 per cent and replace it with fruit. Alternatively all the sugar may be replaced by puréed fruit in which case the cake will not be so light but have a perfectly acceptable, moist texture preferred by many people.

You may use fresh fruit or reconstituted dried fruit. Although fruit can be finely chopped and added to some recipes, it must be puréed before adding if using as a direct substitute for sugar. Use the liquid from the fruit for moistening the cake mixture. Apricots give a good flavour and don't darken the cake as dates, figs or prunes tend to do.

All cakes, especially low sugar ones, are better made with wholemeal(wheat) flour. This gives a better texture and flavour and helps to replace the 'bulk' of the sugar. Self-raising wholemeal(wheat) flour is excellent for cakes and can be used in these recipes, but remember to omit the baking powder.

Decorating Cakes

Avoid 'icing' cakes whenever possible, instead sprinkle with nuts, desiccated coconut, grated cheese or sliced fresh fruit before baking.

If practical, brush the top of the cake with milk, beaten egg, or fruit juice or apple concentrate before baking and again just before end of cooking time.

Mock Icings

● Use puréed fruit, thicken if necessary, with ground almonds or wheatgerm.

● Use cream cheese, curd (Farmer's) cheese or unsweetened peanut butter as a base for spreads. Add puréed fruit, chopped or ground toasted nuts or coconut.

● Use carob instead of cocoa, drinking chocolate or chocolate. It is naturally sweeter (see page 30).

Biscuits and Cookies

The high sugar content is responsible for the 'crispness' of these foods, but by reducing the sugar content and using wholefoods they will still retain some crispness.

Remember: Sugar reduced cakes and biscuits do not keep so well; therefore it is advisable to make in small batches.

Curd Tartlets

(Makes 10)

Fresh or tinned apricots may be used in this recipe.

Imperial/Metric	**American**

Base:

2 oz (55g) butter or margarine, cut up	¼ cup butter or margarine, cut up
4 oz (115g) wholemeal flour	1 cup wholewheat flour
2-2½ tablespoons water	2-2½ tablespoons water

Filling:

1 oz (30g) nuts, finely chopped or ground	¼ cup nuts, finely chopped or ground
10 small dried apricot halves, soaked	10 small dried apricot halves, soaked

Topping:

4 oz (115g) curd cheese	8 tablespoons Ricotta or farmer's cheese
1 oz (30g) butter, melted	2 tablespoons butter, melted
1 egg, beaten	1 egg, beaten
Ground nutmeg	Ground nutmeg

1. Prepare a moderately hot oven 375°F/190°C (Gas Mark 5).

2. Rub butter into flour. Add sufficient water to mix to a firm dough. Knead lightly and roll out thinly. Use to line 10 deep bun or patty tins. Sprinkle nuts over bases.

3. Drain apricots and place one in each case. Reserve juice.

4. Beat cheese, then add butter and beat until smooth. Add egg and about 2 tablespoons apricot juice to make a soft but not runny consistency. Spoon mixture over apricots. Sprinkle tops with nutmeg.

5. Bake in centre of oven for 20-25 minutes until well risen, firm and golden brown. Leave to cool 5 minutes before placing on a cooling tray.

Opposite: From Packed Lunches section: Orangechoc Pudding (page 92), Pizza Quiches (page 85).

Storage:
Best eaten same day. Not suitable for freezing.

To serve:
Warm or cold.

Bread Pudding

An old-time favourite that's moistened and flavoured with carrot and apple.

Imperial/Metric	**American**
¾ lb (340g) stale wholemeal bread, roughly broken	7 cups stale wholewheat bread, roughly broken
½ pint (285ml) warm milk	1⅓ cups warm milk
3 oz (85g) dates, finely chopped	½ cup finely chopped dates
4 oz (115g) currants, raisins, sultanas, mixed	⅔ cup currants, raisins and golden seedless raisins, mixed
1 oz (30g) butter or margarine, chopped	2 tablespoons chopped butter or margarine
2 teaspoons mixed spice	2 teaspoons mixed spice
1 medium-sized carrot, scrubbed	1 medium-sized carrot, scrubbed
1 dessert apple, washed	1 dessert apple, washed
1 egg, beaten	1 egg, beaten

1. Cover bread with cold water. Leave 2 minutes, then drain. Add bread to milk and leave 20 minutes.

2. Prepare a moderate oven 350°F/180°C (Gas Mark 4). Butter a shallow 2-2½ pint (1-1¼ litres/5-6 cups) ovenproof dish or baking tin.

3. Beat bread until smooth. Stir in dates, mixed fruit, butter (margarine) and spice. Finely grate carrot and stir into mixture. Grate apple and beat into mixture with the egg to make a soft consistency.

4. Pour mixture into prepared dish. Bake one hour then reduce heat to 325°F/170°C (Gas Mark 3) for a further one hour or until firm and evenly browned. Cover with greaseproof paper if browning too quickly. Cool in dish.

Storage:
Wrapped in foil in fridge up to 1 week or sliced and frozen up to 2 months.

To serve:
Cold, or warm as a dessert.

Opposite: From Family Cakes section: Golden Pineapple Teabread (page 101), Fig Scones (page 106).

Fig and Almond Bakewell

Either fresh or dried fruit may be used to make a purée for this recipe, but it should not be too moist.

Imperial/Metric	American

Base:

6 oz (170g) wholemeal flour	1½ cups wholewheat flour
3 oz (85g) butter or margarine	⅓ cup butter or margarine
2½-3 tablespoons water	2½-3 tablespoons water

Filling:

4 oz (115g) dried figs, soaked	¾ cup dried figs, soaked

Topping:

3 oz (85g) butter, softened	⅓ cup butter, softened
2 oz (55g) ground almonds	½ cup ground almonds
1 egg, beaten	1 egg, beaten
2 oz (55g) wholemeal flour	½ cup wholewheat flour
1 teaspoon baking powder	1 teaspoon baking powder
Almond essence	Almond essence

Decoration:

Flaked almonds	Slivered almonds

1. Prepare a moderately hot oven 375°F/190°C (Gas Mark 5).

2. *Base:* Rub butter into flour and add sufficient water to mix to a stiff dough. Knead lightly, roll out thinly and use to line a 7 inch (18cm) loose bottomed flan ring.

3. *Filling:* Drain and purée figs. Spread over base of pastry.

4. *Topping:* Cream butter and ground almonds together. Gradually beat in egg. Mix flour and baking powder together and fold into creamed mixture with a few drops of almond essence. Mix to a soft dropping consistency, adding a little fig juice if necessary.

5. Spread mixture carefully over purée. Sprinkle almonds liberally on top. Bake in centre of oven for 25-30 minutes until risen, firm and golden brown. Cool in tin.

Storage:
When cold wrap in foil and keep in the fridge. Eat within 2-3 days, after which time it can be warmed as a dessert. Or freeze up to 2 months.

Orange Raisin Cake

A delicious moist family cake.

Imperial/Metric	**American**
¾ lb (340g) raisins	2 cups raisins
½ pint (285ml) unsweetened orange juice	1⅓ cups unsweetened orange juice
6 oz (170g) butter, softened	⅔ cup butter, softened
2 oz (55g) ground almonds	½ cup ground almonds
3 eggs, beaten	3 eggs, beaten
10 oz (285g) wholemeal flour	2½ cups wholewheat flour
2½ teaspoons baking powder	2½ teaspoons baking powder
1 teaspoon mixed spice	1 teaspoon mixed spice
Grated rind of 1 orange	Grated rind of 1 orange

1. Place raisins and orange juice in a basin and leave overnight.

2. Prepare a moderate oven 350°F/180°C (Gas Mark 4). Grease and line a 7 inch (18cm) round deep-sided cake tin.

3. Beat butter and almonds together. Gradually beat in eggs.

4. Mix flour, baking powder, spice and orange rind together and fold into butter mixture. Add raisins with juice to form a soft dropping consistency, adding juice from orange, if necessary.

5. Place mixture in prepared tin and level top. Bake in centre of oven for 1 hour. Reduce heat to 325°F/170°C (Gas Mark 3) for a further 1-1¼ hours until a skewer comes out clean. Cover with greaseproof paper if browning too quickly. Cool in tin.

Storage:
When cold wrap in foil and eat within 1 week.

Spiced Tea Bread

A moist bread to be sliced and buttered.

Imperial/Metric	**American**
4 oz (115g) All-bran	1½ cups All-bran
1 teaspoon ground cinnamon	1 teaspoon ground cinnamon
½ pint (285ml) warm milk	1⅓ cups warm milk
2 oz (55g) raisins	⅓ cup raisins
2 oz (55g) sultanas	⅓ cup golden seedless raisins
4 oz (115g) wholemeal flour	1 cup wholewheat flour
2 teaspoons baking powder	2 teaspoons baking powder
1 egg, beaten	1 egg, beaten
Unsweetened orange juice to mix	Unsweetened orange juice to mix

1. Place All-bran, cinnamon and milk in a bowl and leave 20 minutes.

2. Prepare a warm oven 325°F/170°C (Gas Mark 3). Grease and line base of 1 lb (455g) loaf tin.

3. Roughly chop raisins and sultanas (golden seedless raisins). Beat All-bran until smooth. Add fruit, flour, baking powder, egg and mix well together, adding a little orange juice if necessary to make a fairly soft dropping consistency.

4. Place mixture in prepared tin. Bake in centre of oven for 1-1¼ hours until firm. Cool in tin.

Storage:
When cold, wrap in foil. Use within 3-4 days and keep in fridge. Or freeze up to 2 months.

Golden Pineapple Teabread

(Makes 1 lb/455g loaf)

Carrot and pineapple give this teabread a good texture and it slices well.

Imperial/Metric	American
6 oz (170g) carrot, finely grated	1 cup finely shredded carrot
½ lb (225g) pineapple, liquidized	1 cup pineapple pieces, liquidized
2 eggs, beaten	2 eggs, beaten
4 tablespoons vegetable oil	4 tablespoons vegetable oil
6 oz (170g) wholemeal flour	1½ cups wholewheat flour
2 teaspoons baking powder	2 teaspoons baking powder
1 teaspoon mixed spice	1 teaspoon mixed spice
1 oz (30g) chopped almonds	¼ cup chopped almonds
1 oz (30g) chopped walnuts	¼ cup chopped English walnuts

Decoration:

2 thin slices pineapple	2 thin slices pineapple
4 walnut halves	4 English walnut halves

1. Prepare a moderate oven 350°F/180°C (Gas Mark 4). Grease and line base of a 1 lb (455g) loaf tin.

2. Place carrots, pineapple, eggs and oil together in a bowl and beat together until well mixed.

3. Mix flour, baking powder, spice, almonds and walnuts together and beat into pineapple mixture. Pour mixture into prepared tin. Halve pineapple slices and arrange over top of loaf with a walnut half in between.

4. Bake in centre of oven for approximately 1¾ hours until firm and a skewer comes out clean. Cool 15 minutes in tin then turn out onto a cooling tray.

Storage:
In fridge 3-4 days or freeze up to 2 months.

To serve:
Sliced thinly with butter, or sliced thickly and toasted.

Dark Banana Buns

(Makes 12)

Mashed banana not only helps to sweeten these buns, but gives a good flavour, too.

Imperial/Metric	American
4 oz (115g) wholemeal flour	1 cup wholewheat flour
2½ teaspoons baking powder	2½ teaspoons baking powder
1 tablespoon carob powder	1 tablespoon carob powder
3 oz (85g) soft margarine	⅓ cup soft margarine
1 tablespoon apple concentrate	1 tablespoon apple concentrate
2 eggs, beaten	2 eggs, beaten
4 oz (115g) peeled ripe banana	1 medium-sized ripe banana, peeled

1. Prepare a moderately hot oven 375°F/190°C (Gas Mark 5). Place 12 paper bun cases in a bun tin.

2. Place flour, baking powder, carob powder, margarine, apple concentrate and eggs in a bowl.

3. Mash banana until smooth and add to bowl. Beat or whisk mixture for 1-2 minutes until light and creamy.

4. Divide mixture between cases, filling each one about two-thirds full. Bake 15-20 minutes until risen and firm to the touch. Cool on a wire tray.

To serve:
Best eaten same day, either warm, or cooled and made into butterfly cakes with Carob Spread (see page 66) or Banana Nut Spread (see page 103) omitting the nuts. Decorate with desiccated coconut or chopped nuts.

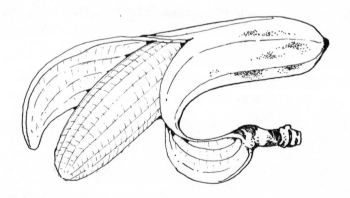

Banana Nut Spread

This makes sufficient to fill or top a 7 inch (18cm) cake.

Imperial/Metric
4 oz (115g) cream cheese
1 small firm, ripe banana
2 teaspoons lemon juice
Milk, to mix
2 oz (55g) finely chopped hazelnuts, toasted

American
8 tablespoons cream cheese
1 small firm, ripe banana
2 teaspoons lemon juice
Milk, to mix
½ cup chopped hazelnuts, toasted

1. Beat cheese until smooth. Mash banana with the lemon juice and beat into cheese, adding a few drops of milk to make a light, fluffy texture.

2. Fold nuts into spread.

Use:
Within 2 hours to prevent discolouration. Not suitable for freezing.

Dark Carob Slices

(Makes 16 slices)

A dark moist cake that the children will love. The dates can be quickly softened by soaking in hot water for half-an-hour with the prunes.

Imperial/Metric	**American**
4 oz (115g) stoned dates, softened	1 cup pitted dates, softened
4 oz (115g) 'ready to serve' prunes, softened	1 cup 'ready to serve' prunes, softened
4 oz (115g) butter, softened	1 cup butter, softened
3 eggs, beaten	3 eggs, beaten
3 oz (85g) wholemeal flour	¾ cup wholewheat flour
1 oz (30g) carob powder	¼ cup carob powder
1 oz (30g) desiccated coconut	⅓ cup desiccated coconut

1. Prepare a moderate oven 350°F/180°C (Gas Mark 4). Grease and line base of an 8 inch (20.5cm) square tin.

2. Drain dates and prunes and place in liquidizer (blender) until smooth. Place in a bowl with the butter and beat until smooth and creamy. Gradually add eggs, beating well between each addition.

3. Mix flour and carob together and fold into creamed mixture. Spread mixture into prepared tin and sprinkle the coconut on top.

4. Bake just above centre of oven for 25-30 minutes until firm. Cool in tin and cut into slices.

Storage:
In fridge 2-3 days or freeze up to 2 months.

To serve:
Warm or cold.

Eve's Drop Scones

(Makes about 14)

To the basic recipe you can add a variety of flavours both sweet and savoury and the scones are just as delicious cold as hot.

Imperial/Metric
4 oz (115g) wholemeal flour
2 teaspoons baking powder
½ teaspoon mixed spice
1 egg, beaten
6 fl oz (170ml) milk and water,
  mixed
Vegetable oil
1 dessert apple, grated

American
1 cup wholewheat flour
2 teaspoons baking powder
½ teaspoon mixed spice
1 egg, beaten
Scant ¾ cup milk and water, mixed
Vegetable oil
1 dessert apple, grated

1. Place flour, baking powder and spice in a bowl. Add egg and half the liquid. Beat until mixture is a smooth batter. Beat in remaining liquid and a tablespoon of oil. (Alternatively use the blender.)

2. Stir the apple into the batter and leave, covered, for 5 minutes.

3. Wipe a heavy-based frying pan or griddle with oil and place over a moderate heat until hot. Using a tablespoon, place a generous spoonful of batter into pan and cook about 2 minutes until scone is just dry on surface. Flip scone over and cook a further one or two minutes. Cook 3 or 4 scones together and keep them warm in a clean tea towel.

To serve:
Warm or cold with butter. Best eaten within a few hours.

Variations:
Replace apple with: Cheese — 2 oz (55g) grated cheese.
Orange — 1 teaspoon grated rind, and use juice instead of milk.
Fruit — 2 tablespoons chopped raisins, or 2 tablespoons puréed fruit.

Fig Scones

(Makes 8-10)

The puréed figs improve both the texture and the flavour of these scones.

Imperial/Metric	American
4 dried figs, soaked	4 dried figs, soaked
6 oz (170g) wholemeal flour	1½ cups wholewheat flour
3 teaspoons baking powder	3 teaspoons baking powder
2 oz (55g) butter, cut up	¼ cup butter, cut up
Milk, to glaze, optional	Milk, to glaze, optional
Crushed wheatflakes, optional	Crushed wheatflakes, optional

1. Prepare a hot oven 425°F/220°C (Gas Mark 7). Lightly dust a baking sheet with flour.

2. Drain and purée figs with 2 fl oz (60ml/¼ cup) fig juice.

3. Place flour, baking powder and butter in a bowl, rub in butter. Add fig purée and sufficient juice to make a fairly soft but not sticky dough. Leave 2 minutes, then knead dough lightly on a floured surface.

4. Flatten dough to a 7 inch (18cm) circle.
   Either: mark into 8 slices with a sharp knife,
   Or: using a 2 inch (5cm) round cutter, cut out circles.

5. Place scones on prepared baking tray. Brush with milk or fig juice and sprinkle wheatflakes over the tops, if used. Bake 10-12 minutes until firm and lightly browned. Cool on a wire tray.

Storage:
Wrap in foil or plastic bag and store in fridge 2-3 days, or freeze up to 2 months.

Variations:
1. Replace figs with 3 oz (85g-½ cup) dried apricots.
2. Replace figs with 3 oz (85g-¾ cup) grated (hard) cheese.

Coconut Biscuits

(Makes about 36)

A good basic biscuit to have in the cupboard.

Imperial/Metric	**American**
6 oz (170g) wholemeal flour	1½ cups wholewheat flour
2 teaspoons baking powder	2 teaspoons baking powder
4 oz (115g) butter, softened	½ cup (1 stick) butter, softened
1 oz (30g) desiccated coconut	⅓ cup desiccated coconut
¼ teaspoon mixed spice	¼ teaspoon mixed spice
4 tablespoons natural yogurt, to mix	4 tablespoons plain yogurt, to mix
Flaked coconut	Flaked coconut

1. Prepare a moderately hot oven 375°F/190°C (Gas Mark 5). Flour two baking sheets.

2. Place flour, baking powder, butter, coconut, spice and sufficient yogurt to mix to a soft dough. Knead lightly on a floured surface until smooth.

3. Roll out to the thickness of pastry. Using a 2 inch (5cm) cutter, cut out biscuits and place on prepared tins. Brush with yogurt, to glaze and sprinkle a little flaked coconut on each biscuit.

4. Bake 15-20 minutes until golden. Cool biscuits on a wire tray.

Storage:
In an airtight tin up to 1 week.

Variation:
Replace desiccated coconut with grated cheese, or chopped raisins.

Peanut Butter Digestives

(Makes 12-14)

These tend to crumble easily so handle with care. Use the Nut Butter recipe on page 88.

Imperial/Metric	**American**
3 oz (85g) wholemeal flour	¾ cup wholewheat flour
1 teaspoon baking powder	1 teaspoon baking powder
2 oz (55g) butter, softened	¼ cup butter, softened
1 tablespoon apple concentrate	1 tablespoon apple concentrate
2 tablespoons peanut butter	2 tablespoons peanut butter
2-3 teaspoons unsweetened fruit juice	2-3 teaspoons unsweetened fruit juice

Decoration:

Chopped peanuts, or sesame seeds	Chopped peanuts, or sesame seeds

1. Prepare a moderate oven 350°F/180°C (Gas Mark 4). Dust a baking sheet with flour.

2. Place flour, baking powder, butter, apple concentrate and peanut butter in a bowl. Mix with a fork, adding a little juice, if necessary, to make a soft dough.

3. Roll out dough thickly. Using a 2 inch (5cm) round cutter, cut out biscuit and lift onto prepared tin. Brush biscuits with juice, to glaze, and sprinkle with chopped peanuts or sesame seeds.

4. Bake 10-15 minutes until golden brown. Lift carefully onto a cooling tray.

Storage:
In an airtight tin 3-4 days.

To serve:
On their own or with cheese. Ideal for crumbling to use as biscuit crumbs in recipes.

7.

FAMILY PUDDINGS

Many people still prefer to end their meal with a pudding although the heavy steamed treacle puds are on the decline. Unfortunately commercially prepared desserts are very popular, yet these contain a high percentage of sugar and only pander to a sweet craving for more sugary foods.

Packet desserts and toppings, jelly, canned fruit in syrup, ice cream and whipped creams should be avoided. Look instead for fruit in natural juice and yogurts with no added sugar or other additives.

Most ice cream recipes are based on a sugar syrup but it is quite simple to reduce this if you make your own, although you may find the texture more granular. Use fresh puréed fruit and replace half the cream with evaporated milk.

Thick set natural (plain) and Greek yogurt make a good substitute for custard or cream.

Fruit

Fruit contains its own sugar (fructose) so it helps to sweeten recipes. The riper the fruit, the sweeter the flavour, and dessert apples, pears and gooseberries are less tart than the cooking varieties. When in season, try fresh pineapples, mangos, kiwi fruit and other exotic fruits, all sweet enough to eat on their own.

Buy sufficient fruit to last only 2-3 days if ripe. Store in a cool dark place, often the fruit bowl on the table is not the ideal place. Fresh fruit makes a quick, refreshing and healthy dessert.

Stewed Fruit

Always sweeten fruit after cooking, to taste. Extra liquid will be required when stewing without sugar so use a few tablespoons unsweetened fruit juice with a knob of butter and simmer over a low heat with a tightly fitting lid on the saucepan.

Sweet Cicely

This is a fern-like herb which helps to reduce the tartness of fruit if added before cooking.

Dried Fruit

These have a concentration of sugar (fructose) but if used sparingly add a valuable source of nutrients and sweetness to the diet. Dates, apricots and the vine fruits are the sweetest. Remember to leave them to soak overnight, or cover with cold water, bring slowly to the boil, remove from heat and leave to soften at least 2 hours — simmer for a few minutes if necessary.

Baked and Steamed Puddings

The same points apply as for cakes (see page 94) but more fruit and less sugar may be used as the light airy texture is not always so necessary in puddings. Steaming is a good method of cooking sugar-related puddings and helps to give a softer texture.

Finish the meal with a sugar-free food such as a small piece of cheese or lemon tea, to clear the palate if brushing the teeth is not possible.

N.B. Apple, although abrasive, does contain natural sugar and is therefore not suitable for this purpose.

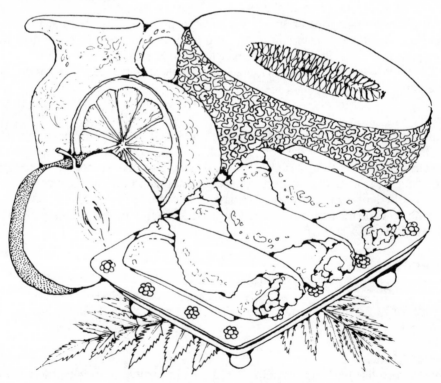

Upside Down Pudding

(Serves 4-6)

Any fresh fruit may be used. Alternatively use canned fruit in natural juice. Drain well and use the juice to make a sauce.

Imperial/Metric	American
1 tablespoon apple concentrate	1 tablespoon apple concentrate
Knob of butter	Knob of butter
1 lb (455g) golden plums, halved and stoned	12 small golden plums, halved and pitted

Topping:

4 oz (115g) wholemeal flour	1 cup wholewheat flour
2 teaspoons baking powder	2 teaspoons baking powder
4 oz (115g) butter, softened	1 stick (½ cup) butter, softened
1½ oz (45g) ground almonds	⅓ cup ground almonds
2 eggs	2 eggs
1 or 2 tablespoons unsweetened fruit juice	1 or 2 tablespoons unsweetened fruit juice

1. Prepare a moderate oven 350°F/180°C (Gas Mark 4). Butter a 2 pint (1 litre/5 cups) shallow ovenproof dish.

2. Mix apple concentrate and butter together and spread over base of dish. Arrange fruit on top.

3. Place flour, baking powder, butter, ground almonds and eggs in a bowl. Beat well until light and fluffy, adding sufficient juice to make a soft, dropping consistency.

4. Dot mixture over fruit and carefully spread to cover. Bake 25-30 minutes until fruit is soft and sponge firm to touch.

To serve:
Warm with custard, natural (plain) yogurt or evaporated milk.

Fruit Crumble

(Serves 4-5)

Imperial/Metric
1½ lb (680g) apples, cored and
  chopped
1 oz (30g) raisins
6 tablespoons unsweetened orange
  juice

American
3 cups chopped apple
¼ cup raisins
6 tablespoons unsweetened orange
  juice

Topping:

3 oz (85g) rolled oats
2 tablespoons melted butter
2 oz (55g) dates, finely chopped
½ teaspoon ground cinnamon
1 tablespoon desiccated coconut or
  sesame seeds or chopped nuts

¾ cup rolled oats
2 tablespoons melted butter
⅓ cup finely chopped dates
½ teaspoon ground cinnamon
1 tablespoon desiccated coconut or
  sesame seeds or chopped nuts

1. Prepare a moderately hot oven 375°F/190°C (Gas Mark 5).

2. Place apples in a 2 pint (1 litre/5 cups) pie dish or equivalent with the raisins
    and juice.

3. Stir oats, butter, dates, cinnamon and coconut (sesame seeds or nuts) together.
    Sprinkle over apples.

4. Bake 30-35 minutes until apples are soft.

To serve:
Hot or cold with custard, natural (plain) yogurt or evaporated milk.

Variations:
Rub 2 oz (55g/¼ cup) butter into 4 oz (115g/1 cup) wholemeal (wheat) flour and
stir in 2 oz (55g/¼ cup) grated (hard) cheese. Sprinkle over fruit.

Stewed Fruit

You need to add a little extra liquid when stewing fruit without sugar.

Dessert varieties of fruit, e.g. gooseberries, apples and pears are less tart than the cooking varieties and young wine rhubarb is better than rhubarb picked later in the season.

Imperial/Metric	**American**
1 lb (455g) ripe fruit	1 pound ripe fruit
8 tablespoons unsweetened apple or orange juice	8 tablespoons unsweetened apple or orange juice
4 'sprigs' sweet cicely, optional	4 'sprigs' sweet cicely, optional
Knob of butter	Knob of butter

1. Wash and prepare fruit, according to kind, leaving skin. Slice fruit and place in a heavy-based pan with the fruit juice, cicely, if used, and butter.

2. Cover pan with a tightly fitting lid and simmer fruit gently until soft.

3. Discard cicely, if used, and taste fruit. Add a few drops apple concentrate or a little fructose, if necessary.

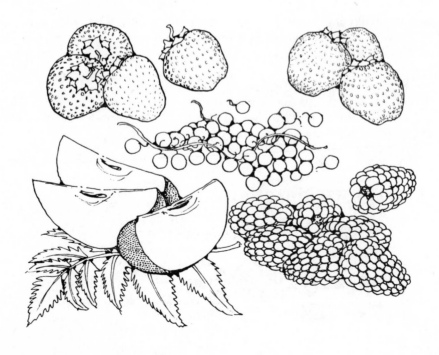

Queen of Puddings

(Serves 4)

Traditionally a very sweet pudding, but this version is just as delicious.

Imperial/Metric	American
½ pint (285ml) milk	1⅓ cups milk
Knob of butter	Knob of butter
Grated rind and juice of ½ lemon	Grated rind and juice of ½ lemon
3 oz (85g) fresh wholemeal breadcrumbs	1½ cups fresh wholewheat breadcrumbs
2 oz (55g) raisins	⅓ cup raisins
2 eggs, separated	2 eggs, separated
1 tablespoon Pear 'n Apple Spread	1 tablespoon Pear 'n Apple Spread
Pinch of sea salt	Pinch of sea salt

1. Bring milk, butter and lemon rind to the boil. Remove from heat and stir in breadcrumbs and raisins. Cover and leave 20 minutes.

2. Prepare a moderate oven 350°F/180°C (Gas Mark 4). Butter a 1½ pint (850ml/3¾ cups) pie dish.

3. Beat egg yolks and lemon juice into mixture and pour it into prepared dish. Bake 20-25 minutes until set and remove from oven. Turn oven up to hot — 425°F/220°C (Gas Mark 7).

4. Dot Pear 'n Apple spread over surface of pudding and carefully spread.

5. Whisk egg whites and salt in a basin over very hot water until stiff. Place meringue over pudding and spread to cover. Return pudding to oven for a few minutes only until golden brown. Serve warm.

Fruit Compote

(Serves 4-6)

Don't let the tea stand too long before pouring it off for this recipe. A speciality tea such as Earl Grey or Orange Blossom gives a delicate flavour.

Imperial/Metric	**American**
½ lb (225g) mixed dried fruit e.g. apricots, figs, prunes, apples	1¾ cups mixed dried fruit e.g. apricots, figs, prunes, apples
¼ pint (140ml) freshly made tea	⅔ cup freshly made tea
½ pint (285g) water	1⅓ cups water
2 inch (5cm) piece cinnamon stick or ¼ teaspoon ground cinnamon	2 inch piece cinnamon stick or ¼ teaspoon ground cinnamon
1 orange	1 orange

1. Place dried fruit, tea, water and cinnamon (stick or ground) in a saucepan. Remove rind from orange with a potato peeler and add to pan.

2. Bring liquid slowly to the boil and remove from heat. Cover and leave 2 or 3 hours or overnight. Simmer fruit 5-10 minutes or until fruit is soft.

3. Discard orange peel and cinnamon stick, if used. Squeeze juice from orange and stir into fruit.

To serve:
Warm or chilled with custard or natural (plain) strained Greek yogurt.

Apricot Steamed Pudding

(Serves 4-6)

A light, moist pudding that may rise less than conventional recipes during cooking.

Imperial/Metric	**American**
2 oz (55g) dried apricots, soaked	⅓ cup dried apricots, soaked
4 oz (115g) stoned dates, soaked	⅔ cup pitted dates, soaked
3 oz (85g) soft margarine or butter, softened	⅓ cup soft margarine or butter, softened
2 eggs, beaten	2 eggs, beaten
4 oz (115g) wholemeal flour	1 cup wholewheat flour
2 teaspoons baking powder	2 teaspoons baking powder
1 teaspoon ground ginger	1 teaspoon ground ginger
2 oz (55g) fresh wholemeal breadcrumbs	1 cup fresh wholewheat breadcrumbs

1. Prepare a steamer. Butter a 1½ pint (850ml/3¾ cup) pudding basin.

2. Drain and purée the apricots and place them in the prepared basin. Reserve juice.

3. Drain and purée the dates. Place in a bowl. Add margarine (butter) and beat until light and fluffy. Gradually beat in eggs.

4. Mix flour, baking powder, ginger and breadcrumbs together and fold into creamed mixture, adding a little juice to make a soft, dropping consistency.

5. Place mixture in basin. Cover and steam 1½-2 hours until firm.

To serve:
Hot with custard or natural (plain) yogurt.

Golden Rice Pudding

(Makes 4 servings)

A more interesting version of the traditional rice pudding.

Imperial/Metric	**American**
1¼ pints (700ml) milk	3⅓ cups milk
Knob of butter	Knob of butter
10 cloves	10 cloves
1 orange	1 orange
2 oz (55g) brown rice	5 tablespoons brown rice
1 oz (30g) sultanas	4 tablespoons golden seedless raisins

1. Prepare a warm oven 325°F/170°C (Gas Mark 3).

2. Place milk, butter and cloves in a saucepan. Wash and remove zest from orange with a potato peeler and add zest to pan. Bring milk to just below boiling point, remove from heat and leave 10 minutes.

3. Place rice and sultanas (golden seedless raisins) in a 1½ pint (850ml-3¾ cup) oven proof dish. Pour milk through a sieve onto rice. Stir well and cook pudding just below centre of oven for 1 hour. Reduce oven temperature to cool 300°F/150°F (Gas Mark 2) for a further 1-1½ hours until all the liquid has been absorbed and grains are soft. Stir occasionally, if desired.

Storage:
In fridge for 3 days or freeze in individual portions up to 2 months.

To serve:
Hot or cold, with the orange flesh.

Crêpes

(Makes 10-12)

Wholemeal(wheat) crêpes can be used with a variety of sweet or savoury fillings.

Imperial/Metric	American
4 oz (115g) wholemeal flour	1 cup wholewheat flour
1 egg	1 egg
Vegetable oil	Vegetable oil
½ pint (285ml) milk and water	1⅓ cups milk and water

1. Place flour, egg, 2 tablespoons vegetable oil and half the liquid in a liquidizer (blender) and run machine until smooth. Add remaining liquid.

2. Using a small heavy-based omelette or frying pan, heat ½ teaspoon of vegetable oil. Pour about 2 tablespoons of batter into pan and swirl round to coat base. Cook 1-2 minutes each side. Flip crêpe onto a plate and repeat with remaining batter.

    Hint: A little extra liquid may be added to the batter if it begins to thicken before all the crêpes have been cooked.

Storage:
Layer crêpes between freezer film and keep in fridge up to 24 hours or freeze up to 6 weeks.

To serve:
Keep crêpes warm on a plate over a pan of hot water. Roll or fold to enclose filling.

Variations:
Orange Crêpes — Stir 2 teaspoons grated orange rind into batter.
Lemon Crêpes — Stir 2 teaspoons grated lemon rind into batter.
Spiced Crêpes — Stir 1 teaspoon ground spice into batter.

Hawaii Rolls

(Serves 4)

Creamed coconut makes a delicious sauce for many desserts. Make this recipe using fresh pineapple whenever possible and unsweetened pineapple juice for the sauce.

Imperial/Metric
8 crêpes (see page 118)
6 slices of pineapple in natural juice

American
8 crêpes (see page 118)
6 slices of pineapple in natural juice

Sauce:

¼ pint (140ml) unsweetened
   pineapple juice
3 oz (85g) creamed coconut
1 tablespoon freshly chopped mint,
   optional

⅔ cup unsweetened pineapple juice
½ block (85g) creamed coconut
1 tablespoon freshly chopped mint,
   optional

1. Warm crêpes over a pan of hot water.

2. Roughly chop pineapple. Measure juice and place with pineapple in a small saucepan. Heat gently. Remove pineapple with a slotted spoon and divide between crêpes. Roll up and place them on a warmed serving dish.

3. Chop coconut, add to pan and stir until dissolved. Remove from heat and beat sauce until it cools and coats back of spoon. Stir in mint, if used.

Storage:
This recipe will not freeze.

To serve:
Pour sauce over crêpes and serve at once. Decorate with extra mint.

Dutch Apple Tart

(Serves 6-8)

The combination of cooking and dessert apples makes this a refreshing dessert.

Imperial/Metric	**American**

Base:

4 oz (115g) wholemeal flour	1 cup wholewheat flour
2 oz (55g) butter, cut up	¼ cup butter, cut up
2 oz (55g) Cheddar cheese, grated	½ cup grated hard cheese

Filling:

1 lb (455g) cooking apples, peeled, cored, sliced	1 pound cooking apples, peeled, cored, sliced
¼ pint (140ml) unsweetened orange juice	⅔ cup unsweetened orange juice
Knob of butter	Knob of butter
¼ teaspoon ground cloves	¼ teaspoon ground cloves

Decoration:

1 large red-skinned dessert apple	1 large red-skinned dessert apple
1 large green-skinned dessert apple	1 large green-skinned dessert apple
½ pint (285ml) unsweetened apple juice	1⅓ cups unsweetened apple juice
1 tablespoon apple concentrate	1 tablespoon apple concentrate

1. Prepare a fairly hot oven 400°F/200°C (Gas Mark 6). Grease an 8 inch (20.5cm) flan ring.

2. *Base:* Place flour in a bowl. Add butter and rub in. Stir in cheese and sufficient water to mix to a soft dough. Knead on a floured surface until smooth. Use to line base and sides of prepared flan ring. Prick base and bake blind 15-20 minutes until golden and base is dry. Cool.

3. *Filling:* Place cooking apples, orange juice, butter and cloves in a saucepan, cover and cook over a low heat until apples are soft. Beat until smooth, cool and chill.

4. Place pastry case on a serving plate and spread apple purée over base.

5. *Decoration:* Wash, core and very thinly slice one dessert apple. Boil apple juice in a large-based pan, for 1 minute then add half the prepared apple, reduce heat and simmer 30 seconds. Remove apple with a draining spoon and place on kitchen (absorbent) paper. Repeat with remaining apple, then slice second apple and repeat. Remove pan from heat.

6. Arrange slices of red and green-skinned apple alternately over puréed apple. Stir apple concentrate into pan, boil until reduced by half or liquid makes a coating consistency. Quickly brush over apple, to glaze. Chill tart until required.

Storage:
Best eaten same day. Do not freeze.

To serve:
Chilled with yogurt or ice cream.

8.

SEASONAL RECIPES

Christmas
Many people find the traditional Christmas cake too rich. Because of the high concentration of dried fruit in the recipe it is possible to make the cake without any other added sugar. The same applies to the mincemeat and pudding recipes. Although flavour and texture are almost identical, they will not keep so long and once matured, must be frozen or kept in the fridge until required.

Decorating the Christmas Cake
Although traditionally the cake is covered in marzipan and royal icing, it is possible to cut down the amount of sugar, yet still produce a Christmassy cake.

- Instead of covering the cake side with marzipan and icing, make a band of foil round the cake to keep it from drying out before covering with a decorative frill.

- Use a low-sugar marzipan recipe and a soft icing which can be spread more thinly than a thick royal icing.

- Instead of icing, place rings of halved walnuts, whole brazils, almonds and hazelnuts on top of cake before baking. Brush nuts after baking with a little apple concentrate or honey, to glaze.

Easter
Simnel cakes and Hot Cross Buns are the only traditional Easter fare still popular. Instead it is a time for children to devour large quantities of chocolate and other sweets in a space of two or three days.

Rules may have to bend a little but it's worth remembering that small eggs contain less chocolate than large ones, and empty eggs are better than filled ones, especially the cream-filled varieties. Carob eggs are available in health food shops for those who prefer not to eat chocolate. Discourage 'nibbling' throughout the day to avoid spoiling appetite and teeth (see chapter Toddler's Teeth on page 46).

Christmas Pudding

(Serves 8)

A moist, fruity pudding that makes a lighter alternative to the traditional.

Imperial/Metric
6 oz (170g) stoned dates, chopped
¼ pint (140ml) unsweetened orange
  juice
4 oz (115g) raisins
2 oz (55g) currants
4 oz (115g) sultanas
3 oz (85g) fresh wholemeal
  breadcrumbs
3 oz (85g) wholemeal flour
2 teaspoons mixed spice
2 oz (55g) butter, chilled and grated
Grated rind of 1 lemon
Grated rind of 1 orange
1 medium-sized carrot, finely grated
1 dessert apple, grated
2 eggs, beaten
3 fl oz (90ml) milk

American
1 cup chopped dates
⅔ cup unsweetened orange juice
⅔ cup raisins
⅓ cup currants
⅔ cup golden seedless raisins
1½ cups fresh wholewheat
  breadcrumbs
¾ cup wholewheat flour
2 teaspoons mixed spice
¼ cup butter, chilled and grated
Grated rind of 1 lemon
Grated rind of 1 orange
1 medium-sized carrot, finely grated
1 dessert apple, grated
2 eggs, beaten
⅓ cup milk

1. Place dates and orange juice in a pan, bring slowly to the boil, then remove from heat. Roughly chop raisins, currants and sultanas (golden seedless raisins), add to dates and leave to cool.

2. Stir breadcrumbs, flour, spice, butter, lemon and orange rind together in a mixing bowl. Add fruit with juice, carrot, apple, eggs and sufficient milk to make a soft dropping consistency. Cover and leave in fridge overnight.

3. Grease a 2 or 2½ pint (1-1¼ litre/5-5¾ cups) pudding basin and two large circles of greaseproof paper. Prepare a steamer.

4. Place mixture in prepared basins, cover with greaseproof paper and muslin. Steam 5 hours.

Storage:
When cold store in fridge up to 2 weeks.

To serve:
Steam a further 2 hours. Serve with custard, natural (plain) yogurt, Greek strained yogurt or Orange Foam Sauce (see page 125).

Christmas Cake

(8 inch/20.5cm round)

Many people don't enjoy the very rich traditional cakes, so this makes a good alternative.

Imperial/Metric
6 oz (170g) stoned dates, chopped
½ pint (285ml) unsweetened apple
    juice
4 oz (115g) currants
4 oz (115g) raisins
4 oz (115g) sultanas
7 oz (200g) butter, softened
2 oz (55g) ground almonds
4 eggs, beaten
2 oz (55g) flaked almonds, crushed
Grated rind of 1 large lemon
1 medium-sized carrot, finely grated
½ teaspoon almond essence
2 teaspoons baking powder
2 teaspoons mixed spice
10 oz (285g) malted wholemeal
    flour*

American
1 cup chopped dates
1⅓ cups unsweetened apple juice
⅔ cup currants
⅔ cup raisins
⅔ cup golden seedless raisins
¾ cup butter, softened
½ cup ground almonds
4 eggs, beaten
½ cup slivered almonds, crushed
Grated rind of 1 large lemon
1 medium-sized carrot, finely grated
½ teaspoon almond essence
2 teaspoons baking powder
2 teaspoons mixed spice
2½ cups malted wholewheat flour*

1. Place dates and apple juice in a pan. Bring slowly to the boil, remove from heat and stir in currants, raisins and sultanas (golden seedless raisins). Cover and leave until cold or overnight.

2. Prepare a warm oven 325°F/170°C (Gas Mark 3). Grease and line an 8 inch (20.5cm) deep round cake tin.

3. Cream butter and ground almonds together until light. Gradually add eggs, beating between each addition. Fold in crushed almonds, lemon rind, carrot and almond essence.

4. Stir baking powder and spice into flour. Add half the flour to the creamed mixture with half the fruit. Carefully fold in and repeat with remaining ingredients to make a soft, dropping consistency.

5. Place mixture in prepared tin and level top. Bake in centre of oven as follows:

*Use wholemeal(wheat) flour if malted variety is unobtainable.

1st hour: 325°F/170°C (Gas Mark 3).
2nd hour: 275°F/140°C (Gas Mark 1).
Extra ½ hour: lowest setting.

Cover cake with greaseproof if browning too quickly. Test with a skewer after 2 hours.

6. Cool cake in tin.

Storage:
Do not remove greaseproof, but wrap cake well in foil until ready to use or leave 2-3 days to mature and then freeze. Thaw 2 days before use.

Orange Foam Sauce

(Makes about ¾ pint/425ml/2 cups)

Use this sauce with Christmas Pudding or recipes in the Family Pudding chapter.

Imperial/Metric	**American**
Juice from 2 large oranges	Juice from 2 large oranges
2 teaspoons grated orange rind	2 teaspoons grated orange rind
1 egg, separated	1 egg, separated
2 teaspoons arrowroot	2 teaspoons arrowroot

1. Make juice up to ½ pint (285ml/1⅓ cups) with water, if necessary. Warm gently with the rind.

2. Cream yolk and arrowroot together in a basin, gradually add juice, stirring continuously. Return juice to saucepan and stir over a low heat until sauce thickens and coats back of spoon. Cool slightly.

3. Whisk egg white until just thick. Fold into sauce and pour into a serving dish.

To serve:
Warm. Sauce will separate if allowed to cool.

Mincemeat

(Makes about 2 lb/900g)

Originally derived from a savoury recipe, the present traditional version has so much fruit it doesn't need the added sweetness of sugar.

Imperial/Metric	**American**
4 oz (115g) currants	⅔ cup currants
4 oz (115g) raisins	⅔ cup raisins
4 oz (115g) sultanas	⅔ cup golden seedless raisins
3 oz (85g) stoned dates, chopped	½ cup stoned dates, chopped
2 dessert apples, grated	2 dessert apples, grated
1 medium-sized carrot, finely grated	1 medium-sized carrot, finely grated
Grated rind and juice of 1 large lemon	Grated rind and juice of 1 large lemon
2 oz (55g) flaked almonds, crushed	½ cup slivered almonds, crushed
1 oz (30g) butter, chilled and grated or finely chopped	2 tablespoons butter, chilled and grated or finely chopped
2 teaspoons mixed spice	2 teaspoons mixed spice
1 or 2 tablespoons brandy	1 or 2 tablespoons brandy

1. Mince currants, raisins, sultanas (golden seedless raisins) and dates together into a mixing bowl.

2. Add apples, carrot, lemon rind and juice, almonds, butter, spice and brandy. Mix thoroughly. Cover and leave in fridge overnight. Alternatively, this recipe may be made in the food processor.

Storage:
Place mincemeat in sterilized jars, seal and keep in the fridge up to 2 weeks.

Use:
Mince pies, Festive Slices (see page 130).

Truffles

(Makes 12 petit fours)

Fresh breadcrumbs make a suitable base for these cakes. Alternatively, for a richer mixture use cake crumbs (see Family Cake chapter).

Imperial/Metric	American
1 bar (60g) orange flavoured block carob	1 bar orange flavored block carob
1 oz (30g) butter	2 tablespoons butter
2 oz (55g) fresh wholemeal breadcrumbs	1 cup fresh wholewheat breadcrumbs
1 oz (30g) ground almonds	¼ cup ground almonds
1 teaspoon grated orange rind	1 teaspoon grated orange rind
1 teaspoon grated lemon rind	1 teaspoon grated lemon rind
1 oz (30g) flaked almonds, crushed	¼ cup slivered almonds, crushed
1 oz (30g) raisins, chopped	2 tablespoons raisins, chopped
2 tablespoons rum	2 tablespoons rum
Orange juice, to mix	Orange juice, to mix
Ground desiccated coconut, ground nuts, or sesame seeds	Ground desiccated coconut, ground nuts, or sesame seeds

1. Melt carob and butter in a basin over hot water or in the microwave oven.

2. Stir in breadcrumbs, ground almonds, orange and lemon rind, almonds, raisins and rum. Add sufficient orange juice to mix to a soft dough. Chill ½ hour.

3. Divide mixture into twelve pieces and mould each into a ball. Roll truffles in coconut, nuts or sesame seeds, to coat. Chill. Serve in petit fours cases.

Simnel Cake

(7 inch/18cm round)

A traditional spiced cake that has a layer of Almond Paste (see page 131) cooked inside.

Imperial/Metric	American
4 oz (115g) dried apricots, chopped	⅔ cup chopped dried apricots
7 fl oz (200ml) unsweetened orange juice	¾ cup unsweetened orange juice
2 oz (55g) raisins	⅓ cup raisins
2 oz (55g) currants	⅓ cup currants
4 oz (115g) sultanas	⅔ cup golden seedless raisins
6 oz (170g) butter, softened	1½ sticks (¾ cup) butter, softened
2 oz (55g) ground almonds	½ cup ground almonds
3 eggs, beaten	3 eggs, beaten
Grated rind of 1 large lemon	Grated rind of 1 large lemon
2 oz (55g) flaked almonds, crushed	½ cup flaked almonds, crushed
¼ teaspoon almond essence	¼ teaspoon almond essence
10 oz (285g) malted wholemeal flour*	2½ cups malted wholewheat flour*
2 teaspoons baking powder	2 teaspoons baking powder
1 teaspoon mixed spice	1 teaspoon mixed spice
1 teaspoon cinnamon	1 teaspoon cinnamon
½ recipe Almond Paste (see page 131)	½ recipe Almond Paste (see page 131)

1. Place apricots and orange juice in a pan, bring slowly to the boil. Remove from heat and stir in raisins, currants, and sultanas (golden seedless raisins). Leave to cool or overnight.

2. Grease and line 7 inch (18cm) round deep sided cake tin. Prepare a moderate oven 350°F/180°C (Gas Mark 4).

3. Cream butter and ground almonds together until smooth. Gradually add eggs, beating well between each addition. Fold in lemon rind, crushed almonds and almond essence.

4. Mix flour, baking powder, mixed spice and cinnamon together. Fold half the flour and half the fruit into the creamed mixture. Repeat with remaining ingredients to make a soft, dropping consistency.

Opposite: From Family Puddings section: Dutch Apple Tart (page 120), Fruit Crumble (page 112).

5. Place half the mixture into the prepared tin and level. Roll out Almond Paste to a 7 inch (18cm) circle and place in tin. Spread remaining cake mixture on top.

6. Bake in centre of oven as follows:

1st hour: 350°F/180°C (Gas Mark 4).
2nd hour: 300°F/150°C (Gas Mark 2).
Extra time: lowest setting.

Cover with greaseproof paper if cake is browning too quickly. Test with a skewer after 1¾ hours. Cool in tin.

Storage:
Do not remove paper, but wrap cake well in foil. Use within 2 weeks or leave 2-3 days to mature before freezing. Thaw 2-3 days before use.

*Use wholemeal(wheat) flour if malted variety is not available.

Traditional Decoration

The eleven eggs represent the faithful apostles.

Roll 6 oz (170g) Almond Paste (see page 131) into a 7 inch (18cm) circle. Place a 5 inch (13cm) saucer upside down in centre and cut round. Carefully lift up outer ring and place on top of cake. Use small circle to make eleven small eggs and place round edge of cake. Place cake under a medium-hot grill (broiler) for a few seconds until Almond Paste begins to brown. Remove immediately. Place a few Easter chicks in centre of cake and a strip of foil round side of cake before fixing a traditional frill in place.

Opposite: From Seasonal Recipes section: Hot Cross Buns (page 132), Chocolate Nests (page 133) with Almond Paste Eggs (page 131).

Festive Slices

(Makes 12 slices)

Use the Almond Paste and Mincemeat recipes on page 131 and 126 for this delicious alternative to mince pies.

Imperial/Metric   **American**

Pastry:

6 oz (170g) wholemeal flour   1½ cups of wholewheat flour
1 teaspoon baking powder   1 teaspoon baking powder
3 oz (85g) butter or margarine, cut   ⅓ cup butter or margarine, cut up
  up   1 small egg, beaten
1 small egg, beaten   ⅓ cup cold water
3 fl oz (90ml) cold water

Filling:

½ quantity Almond Paste   ½ quantity Almond Paste
8 rounded tablespoons Mincemeat   8 rounded tablespoons Mincemeat
1 oz (30g) flaked almonds   ¼ cup slivered almonds
Milk or egg, to glaze   Milk or egg, to glaze

1. Prepare a fairly hot oven 400°F/200°C (Gas Mark 6). Grease a shallow 7 inch (18cm) square tin.

2. *Pastry:* Place flour and baking powder in a bowl. Add butter or margarine and rub into flour. Add egg and sufficient cold water to mix to a soft dough. Turn dough onto a well-floured surface and knead lightly until smooth. Use two-thirds of the pastry to line prepared tin.

3. *Filling:* Lightly flatten or roll Almond Paste and press onto base of pastry. Spread Mincemeat on top. Using remaining pastry, cut thin strips and position pastry diagonally at intervals across mincemeat, sealing ends well and glaze with milk or egg. Sprinkle almonds liberally over tart.

4. Bake 25-30 minutes until pastry is cooked and golden. Leave at least 5 minutes in tin before cutting into slices.

Storage:
Wrapped in foil 4-5 days in fridge, or freeze up to 3 months.

To serve:
Cold or warm with custard or yogurt.

Almond Paste

(Makes about ¾ lb/340g)

Use for covering cakes, making petits fours, novelty shapes, stuffing dates, and Festive Slices (see page 130).

Imperial/Metric	American
½ pint (285ml) unsweetened apple or orange juice	1⅓ cups unsweetened apple or orange juice
2 oz (55g) wholemeal semolina	½ cup wholewheat semolina
1 teaspoon almond essence	1 teaspoon almond essence
4 oz (115g) ground almonds	1 cup ground almonds
Extra ground almonds for rolling	Extra ground almonds for rolling

1. Place apple or orange juice in a small saucepan and bring to the boil. Add semolina and stir continuously over a medium heat until mixture thickens and begins to leave side of pan. Remove from heat. Cover and cool. Leave in fridge until cold.

2. Beat in almond essence and ground almonds to make a soft dough. Knead lightly until smooth. Chill.

3. Using extra ground almonds, lightly roll out paste as required.

Storage:
Wrap loosely in greaseproof paper and keep in fridge up to 1 week.

N.B. Not suitable for covering with icing.

Hot Cross Buns

(Makes 16)

Use easy-blend dried yeast which is simply stirred into the dry ingredients for easy mixing.

Imperial/Metric	American
1 lb (455g) malted brown flour*	4 cups malted brown flour*
3 oz (85g) butter, cut up	⅓ cup butter, cut up
1 sachet Easy Blend dried yeast (equivalent ½ oz/15g)	1 sachet Easy Blend dried yeast (equivalent to 1 tablespoon)
1 teaspoon mixed spice	1 teaspoon mixed spice
1 teaspoon ground cinnamon	1 teaspoon ground cinnamon
3 oz (85g) currants	½ cup currants
3 oz (85g) sultanas	½ cup golden seedless raisins
Grated rind of 1 large lemon	Grated rind of 1 large lemon
1 egg, beaten	1 egg, beaten
½ pint (285ml) warm milk and water	1⅓ cups warm milk and water
Beaten egg, to glaze	Beaten egg, to glaze

1. Place flour in a large bowl, add butter and rub in. Stir in yeast, spice, cinnamon, currants, sultanas (golden seedless raisins) and lemon rind.

2. Beat egg into milk/water, pour all at once onto dry ingredients and beat until well mixed. (Mixture will appear quite wet at this stage.) Beat dough hard for 5 minutes until mixture begins to leave sides of bowl clean. Cover bowl with oiled plastic and leave in a warm place for about 1 hour or until dough has doubled in size.

3. Turn dough onto a floured surface and knead hard for at least 5 minutes. Cut dough in half and each piece into eight. Knead each piece into a smooth ball and place on a floured baking sheet. Flatten each bun slightly, cover tray loosely with oiled plastic and leave in a warm place for about 20 minutes or until buns have doubled in size.

4. Prepare a fairly hot oven 400°F/200°C (Gas Mark 6).

5. Brush buns with beaten egg, to glaze, and decorate with a cross, if desired (see below). Bake just above centre of oven for 15-20 minutes until golden brown.

*If malted brown flour (Granary) is unobtainable use wholemeal (wheat) flour or 85 per cent extraction.

Storage:
Wrap and keep in fridge 24 hours or freeze up to 3 months.

To serve:
Warm, cold or halved and toasted.

To decorate with a cross:
Use very thin strips of pastry or Almond Paste (see page 131), and stick onto each bun with egg. Alternatively, cut a small cross on the top of each bun before leaving to rise.

Chocolate Nests

(Makes 6)

These make a healthier alternative to Easter eggs.

Imperial/Metric	**American**
1 oz (30g) butter	2 tablespoons butter
1 bar (60g) orange flavoured carob block	1 bar orange flavored carob block
2 Shredded Wheat, crushed	2 Shredded Wheat, crushed

1. Place six paper bun cases in a patty tin.

2. Melt butter and carob in a basin over hot water or in the microwave oven. Stir in Shredded Wheat, to coat.

3. Divide mixture between paper cases and lightly press a well in the centre of each. Chill until set.

Fill centres with:
1. Almond Paste eggs (see page 131). (Eggs must be stored in the refrigerator.)
2. Sugar-free yogurt-coated raisins or similar.

9.

ENTERTAINING

It's tempting to feel that it can do no harm to indulge in rich sugary foods now and again. And when better than entertaining. It is possible, however, that many people actually don't like these kinds of desserts and would prefer a refreshing fruit salad to the elaborate gâteau that took so long and was so expensive to make.

Nouvelle Cuisine is a popular idea now on the Continent introducing the concept of very small portions. The idea being that the individual can choose exactly how much or little they wish to eat as well as how many other flavours or desserts they wish to try. Perhaps we should adopt this way when serving our desserts, certainly it is advisable to make two different kinds to cater for everyone's preferences.

Any of the following ideas can be served as family puddings, but are special enough for more mature palates.

Pre-whipped creams have added sugar, but the Greek strained, thick set yogurt has the smooth consistency of cream that many may prefer. One or two tablespoons of a liqueur may be added to any dessert for that special flavour, and it is a good idea to serve chilled freshly squeezed fruit juices or a fruit cocktail for those who prefer a non-alcoholic drink.

Fromage Blanc

(Serves 6)

This is a light, refreshing cheese dessert to serve with raspberries, or other fresh fruit. It should be made the day before serving.

Imperial/Metric	American
6 oz (170g) cream cheese	⅔ cup soft cream cheese
1 small egg, separated	1 small egg, separated
1 teaspoon finely grated lemon rind	1 teaspoon finely grated lemon rind
¼ pint (140ml) thick set natural yogurt	⅔ cup thick set plain yogurt

1. Place cheese in a bowl and beat until smooth, add egg yolk and lemon rind and continue beating until well blended.

2. Gradually beat in yogurt.

3. Whisk egg white until stiff and fold into cheese mixture.

4. Line a small nylon or plastic sieve with muslin or white kitchen paper (paper towel) and place sieve over a basin. Spoon the cheese mixture into the sieve and cover with muslin (paper). Place in the fridge overnight.

Storage:
Up to 24 hours in fridge. Do not freeze.

To serve:
Remove muslin (paper) from top and invert sieve onto a small plate. Carefully remove muslin (paper) and return mould to fridge until required. Serve with fresh fruit.

Cashew Sorbet

(Makes 1 pint/570ml/2½ cups)

An unusual combination of ground (unsalted) cashew nuts and pineapple juice, but you do need a liquidizer (blender) to make it.

Imperial/Metric	**American**
4 oz (115g) shelled cashew nuts	1 cup shelled cashew nuts
½ pint (285ml) unsweetened pineapple juice	1⅓ cups unsweetened pineapple juice
2 tablespoons lemon juice	2 tablespoons lemon juice
¼ teaspoon ground ginger	¼ teaspoon ground ginger
2 egg whites	2 egg whites

1. Place nuts, pineapple juice, lemon juice and ground ginger in a liquidizer (blender) and run machine until mixture is smooth and creamy. Pour into a freezer container, cover with foil and freeze until mixture begins to freeze round edges. Chill a large bowl.

2. Whisk egg whites until stiff. Turn sorbet into chilled bowl and whisk or beat until smooth. Quickly fold in egg whites and return sorbet to freezer, covered, for 1 hour or until frozen.

To serve:
Place sorbet in fridge about 50 minutes before serving. Serve in small portions with slices of fresh pineapple or fresh cherries.

Apricot Crêpes

(Serves 6 — makes 12 × 6 inch/15.5cm crêpes)

The crêpes can be made in advance and re-heated in the sauce. Use fresh apricots, if available (see note).

Imperial/Metric	**American**

Crêpes:

4 oz (115g) wholemeal flour	1 cup wholewheat flour
1 teaspoon ground cinnamon	1 teaspoon ground cinnamon
1 egg	1 egg
Vegetable oil	Vegetable oil
½ pint (285ml) milk/water	1⅓ cups milk/water

Sauce:

1 × 14 oz (395g) can apricots in natural juice	2 cups canned apricots in natural juice
1 oz (30g) butter	2 tablespoons butter
Rind and juice of 1 large orange	Rind and juice of 1 large orange
2 tablespoons brandy	2 tablespoons brandy
1 tablespoon lemon juice	1 tablespoon lemon juice
1 oz (30g) flaked almonds, toasted	¼ cup slivered almonds, toasted

1. *Crêpes:* Place flour, cinnamon, egg, 2 tablespoons oil and half the milk/water in a liquidizer (blender) and run machine until smooth. Add remaining liquid. Make crêpes as instructions on page 118.

2. *Sauce:* Drain apricots and reserve juice. Roughly chop apricots, divide between crêpes and fold each one in four like a fan.

3. Melt butter, add apricot juice, orange rind and juice. Bring to the boil, reduce heat and cook 1 minute. Stir in brandy and lemon juice. Add crêpes and simmer gently 1 minute, spooning sauce over, to coat.

Storage:
Layer the unfilled crêpes between freezer film and freeze up to six weeks, or store in fridge up to 24 hours.

To serve:
Place crêpes on a warmed serving dish, drizzle sauce over and sprinkle nuts on top. Serve at once.

N.B. When available use 6 fresh apricots halved and simmer in ¼ pint (140ml/ ⅔ cup) unsweetened apple juice.

Chocolate Pots

(Serves 6)

This recipe is quite rich so serve in small quantities.

Imperial/Metric	**American**
6 oz (170g) cream cheese	12 tablespoons cream cheese
1 egg, separated	1 egg, separated
2 teaspoons grated orange rind	2 teaspoons grated orange rind
1½ bars (90g) orange flavoured block carob	1½ bars orange flavored carob bar
2 tablespoons Grand Marnier	2 tablespoons Grand Marnier
¼ pint (140ml) double cream	⅔ cup heavy cream

Decoration:

Whipped cream or Greek yogurt	Whipped cream or Greek yogurt
Carob slivers	Carob slivers

1. Beat cheese until smooth, add egg yolk and orange rind, and mix well together.

2. Melt carob over hot water or in a microwave oven. Stir into cheese with Grand Marnier.

3. Lightly whip cream and egg white separately, carefully fold cream, then egg white into mixture.

4. Divide between 6 individual pots or glasses. Chill.

To serve:
Place a small spoonful of cream or yogurt on each and top with slivers of carob.

Tutti Frutti

(Serves 5-6)

This can be made with all cream but tends to be very rich, so the thick set yogurt helps to balance this. Serve in small portions, sherry glasses are ideal. For a low-fat dessert replace cream with yogurt and fold in all the ingredients carefully.

Imperial/Metric	**American**
¼ pint (140ml) double cream	⅔ cup heavy cream
¼ pint (140ml) strained Greek yogurt, stirred	⅔ cup strained Greek yogurt, stirred
1 tablespoon brandy, optional	1 tablespoon brandy, optional
1 oz (30g) sesame seeds, toasted	¼ cup sesame seeds, toasted
1 oz (30g) medium oatmeal, toasted	¼ cup medium oatmeal, toasted
2 oz (55g) chopped nuts, toasted	½ cup chopped nuts, toasted
½ dessert apple, finely chopped	½ dessert apple, finely chopped
20 red cherries, stoned	20 red cherries, pitted

1. Whip cream until just thick. Gradually whisk in yogurt and brandy and continue whisking until thick.

2. Lightly fold in sesame seeds, oatmeal, nuts and apple. Finely chop cherries and fold into cream. Divide between small glasses. Leave in fridge for at least one hour before serving.

Storage:
Use within 6 hours.

To serve:
With Peanut Digestives (see page 108).

Citrus Trifle

(Serves 6)

This dessert must be made several hours in advance to allow the juice to soak through to the crumbs.

Imperial/Metric

2 oz (55g) butter
3 oz (85g) wholemeal breadcrumbs
Rind and juice of 2 medium-sized
   oranges
Rind and juice of 1 lemon
½ pint (285ml) double cream
¼ pint (140ml) thick set Greek
   yogurt

American

¼ cup butter
1½ cups wholewheat breadcrumbs
Rind and juice of 2 medium-sized
   oranges
Rind and juice of 1 lemon
1⅓ cups heavy cream
⅔ cup thick set Greek yogurt

1. Melt butter, add crumbs and stir over a low heat until crumbs are golden. Divide between six ramekin dishes or place in a 1½ pint (850ml-3¾ cups) serving bowl.

2. Reserve rind from 1 orange for decoration and wrap in clingfilm to keep fresh. Measure lemon and orange juice to 6 fl oz (170ml-just over ⅔ cup).

3. Whisk cream until just thick, gradually add juice and continue whisking until all has been incorporated. Gradually whisk in yogurt. (Do not worry if cream begins to slacken at this stage.) Stir in grated rinds.

4. Pour cream over crumbs and place in fridge for at least 4 hours until cream has become firm.

Storage:
In fridge up to 8 hours — will not freeze.

To serve:
Decorate with reserved rind.

Strawberry Flan

(Serves 6-8)

Use sliced kiwi fruit when strawberries are out of season.

Imperial/Metric	**American**

Pastry:

4 oz (115g) wholemeal flour	1 cup wholewheat flour
2 oz (55g) butter, cut up	¼ cup butter, cut up
1 oz (30g) almonds, finely chopped	¼ cup finely chopped almonds
3 tablespoons water	3 tablespoons water

Custard:

¼ pint (140ml) milk	⅔ cup milk
Grated rind of ½ orange	Grated rind of ½ orange
1 egg yolk	1 egg yolk
1 tablespoon arrowroot	1 tablespoon arrowroot
¼ pint (140ml) single cream	⅔ cup light cream
1 teaspoon almond essence	1 teaspoon almond essence

Topping:

½ lb (225g) strawberries	½ pound strawberries
Juice of 1 large orange	Juice of 1 large orange
1 teaspoon vegetable gel	1 teaspoon vegetable gel

1. Prepare fairly hot oven 400°F/200°C (Gas Mark 6). Grease an 8 inch (20.5cm) flan ring.

2. Place flour in a bowl, add butter and rub in. Stir in almonds and sufficient water to make a soft dough. Knead lightly on a floured surface until smooth. Use pastry to line base and sides of prepared flan ring. Prick base and bake blind for 15-20 minutes, until golden brown and base is firm. Leave to cool.

3. Warm milk and orange rind. Blend egg yolk and arrowroot together and gradually add milk, stirring continuously. Return milk to pan and add cream, stirring over a low heat until sauce thickens. Remove from heat and stir in almond essence. Chill.

4. Place pastry case on a flat serving plate and spread custard over base. Slice the strawberries and arrange over custard.

5. Make orange juice up to ½ pint (285ml/1⅓ cups) with water and strain through muslin or kitchen paper, to clear. Warm juice, sprinkle in vegetable gel and stir until dissolved, remove from heat and continue stirring until gel begins to thicken. Quickly pour over the strawberries to cover. Chill tart until ready to serve.

Storage:
Best eaten same day. Do not freeze.

To serve:
Chilled with yogurt.

N.B. If gel sets too quickly, gently re-heat.

Avocado and Coconut Creams

(Serves 6-8)

A delicious rich dessert combining two unusual flavours. The avocado pear must be ripe, but not over-ripe, for perfect flavour.

Imperial/Metric	American
Rind and juice of 1 large orange	Rind and juice of 1 large orange
2 oz (55g) creamed coconut, chopped	⅓ packet creamed coconut, chopped
2 small ripe avocado pears	2 small ripe avocado pears
¼ pint (140ml) single cream	⅔ cup light cream
1 tablespoon lemon juice	1 tablespoon lemon juice
2 oz (55g) butter	¼ cup butter
3 oz (85g) fresh wholemeal breadcrumbs	1½ cups fresh wholewheat breadcrumbs
2 oz (55g) finely chopped walnuts	½ cup finely chopped English walnuts

To decorate:

Flaked coconut	Flaked coconut
Orange slices	Orange slices

1. Make orange juice up to 3 fl oz (90ml/⅓ cup) with water, if necessary and heat gently. Stir in coconut until dissolved. Remove from heat, cool and chill several hours until thick.

2. Halve and remove stones from avocados, scoop out flesh and place in a liquidizer with the coconut, 2 teaspoons orange rind, cream and lemon juice. Run machine until smooth and well blended. Cover and chill.

3. Melt butter in a saucepan, add breadcrumbs and stir over a moderate heat until evenly browned. Cool.

To serve:
Layer the nuts, breadcrumbs and avocado mixture alternately in serving glasses. Decorate with flaked coconut and an orange slice. Return to fridge, covered, and serve within 1 hour.

Exotic Fruit Salad

(Serves 6-8)

Make this salad two to three hours in advance to allow the flavours to blend. Vary the fruits according to availability.

Imperial/Metric
1 large orange
½ honeydew melon
2 large sprigs of fresh mint
¾ lb (340g) strawberries
3 kiwi fruit (Chinese gooseberry)
Juice of 1 large orange

American
1 large orange
½ honeydew melon
2 large sprigs of fresh mint
¾ pound strawberries
3 kiwi fruit (Chinese gooseberry)
Juice of 1 large orange

1. Cut away skin and pith from orange. Cut out flesh segments, halve and place in a large bowl.

2. Using a small melon scoop, cut out balls of melon and add to orange with one sprig of mint.

3. Hull and slice strawberries. Peel and thickly slice kiwi fruits (Chinese gooseberries). Halve kiwi slices and add to bowl with strawberries and remaining mint. Pour over orange juice.

4. Cover bowl tightly with clingfilm and leave at room temperature for 1 hour. Lightly toss salad, re-cover and place in the fridge until required.

To serve:
Remove mint and replace with a few fresh leaves. Serve chilled, either in the melon skin(s) or in a bowl surrounded by ice.

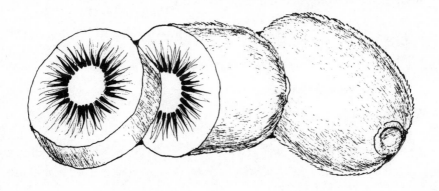

Caraway Crackers

(Makes about 30)

These can be served with pre-dinner drinks and with cheese at the end of the meal.

Imperial/Metric	American
2 oz (55g) wholemeal flour	½ cup wholewheat flour
2 tablespoons medium oatmeal	2 tablespoons medium oatmeal
1 oz (30g) butter, cut up	2 tablespoons butter, cut up
1 tablespoon caraway seeds	1 tablespoon caraway seeds
2½-3 tablespoons milk	2½-3 tablespoons milk

1. Prepare a moderately hot oven 375°F/190°C (Gas Mark 5). Dust 2 baking sheets with flour.

2. Place flour and oatmeal in a bowl, add butter and rub in. Stir in caraway seeds and sufficient milk to make a soft dough. Knead lightly on a floured surface until smooth.

3. Roll out very thinly. Using a 1½ inch (4cm) cutter, cut out biscuits and place on prepared baking sheets. Bake just above centre of oven for 15-20 minutes until golden all over. Cool on wire tray.

Storage:
In an airtight tin for one week.

To serve:
Serve with drinks, cheese or fruit.

Variation:
Use sesame seeds to replace the caraway seeds.

10.

SHOPPING GUIDE FOR LOW-SUGAR PRODUCTS

A Few 'No Added Sugar' and 'Reduced Sugar' Products Available
It is only possible to mention a few of the major Food Groups and Supermarkets with these special ranges and the list is in no way intended to be complete.

New products are continually being introduced and you should look out for these in your local shops.

BABY FOODS

No Added Sugar

COW & GATE

Drinks:
Pure Juice with Vitamin C
Pure Concentrated Juice with Vitamin C

Stage 1: **Strained Desserts**
Apple Dessert
Apple and Banana Dessert
Apple and Orange Dessert
Fruit Delight Dessert

Stage 2: **Junior**
Apple Dessert
Apple and Banana Dessert
Apple and Orange Dessert
Fruit Delight Dessert
Pineapple Dessert

BOOTS BABY FOODS

Breakfast Porridge Oats
Mixed Cereal Breakfast
Protein Baby Cereal
Baby Rice

MILUPA

Cheese and Apple Treat
Infant Drink
Junior Drink
Pure Rice Cereal

HEINZ

All Pure Fruit varieties in cans and jars.

Strained Cans
Pear Dessert

Junior Cans
Apple Dessert and Cream
Banana Rice and Rosehip
Fruit Dessert and Tapioca

Dessert Jars
Pineapple Dessert with Vitamin C

Baby Yogurts
Muesli

ROBINSONS

Baby Rice

Breakfast Cereals
Corn Rice and Barley Malt
Mixed Cereal
Porridge Oats

Breakfast Cereals with Fruit
Apples and Pear
Muesli
Orange and Banana

Baby Juices
All varieties

Low in Sugar (compared with standard products)

COW & GATE
Liga Rusks

BOOTS

Granulated Baby Foods
Oat Breakfast
Mixed Cereal with Wholewheat and Wheatgerm
Porridge Oats with Malt
Apple and Blackberry Treat
Orange and Banana Dessert

Rusks
Low-Sugar Rusks
Low-Sugar Apricot Flavour Rusks

Reduced in Sugar (compared with standard products)

MILUPA
Muesli Rusks
Fruit Rusks

GENERAL FOODS

No Added Sucrose

NESTLE

Evaporated Milk
Sterilized Cream
Custard Powder

LIBBY

Grapefruit Juice Unsweetened
Evaporated Milk
Orange Juice Unsweetened

Pineapple Juice
Tomato Juice

Fruits in Natural Juice
Chunky Mixed Fruits
Peach Halves or Slices
Pear Halves

St. Ivel 'Real' Yogurts and Fruit Juices

Reduced in Sugar (compared with standard products)

BOOTS

Reduced Sugar Apricot Jam
Reduced Sugar Blackcurrant Jam
Reduced Sugar Orange Marmalade
Reduced Sugar Strawberry Jam

HEINZ Weight Watchers

Reduced Sugar Apricot Jam
Reduced Sugar Blackcurrant Jam
Reduced Sugar Raspberry Jam
Reduced Sugar Strawberry Jam
Reduced Sugar Thin Cut Orange Marmalade

CROSSE & BLACKWELL

Baked Beans (25 per cent less sugar)

Low-Sugar

Robinsons Special 'R' Fruit Drinks

Orange
Orange and Pineapple

OWN LABEL SUPERMARKET BRANDS

SAFEWAY

Foods with 'No Added Sugar'

Jams and Marmalades
No Added Sugar Apricot Jam
No Added Sugar Blackcurrant Jam
No Added Sugar Orange Marmalade
No Added Sugar Raspberry Jam
No Added Sugar Strawberry Jam

Fruits (canned)
*Fruit Cocktail in Fruit Juice
*Peaches in Fruit Juice
*Pears in Fruit Juice
Pineapple in Natural Juice

Cereals
Hot Oat Cereal
Quick Cooking Oats
*Rough Oat Cakes
35 per cent Fruit and Nut Muesli

Drinks
Long Life Unsweetened Apple Juice
Long Life Freshly Pressed English Apple Juice
Long Life Unsweetened Grapefruit Juice
Long Life Unsweetened Orange Juice
Long Life Unsweetened Pineapple Juice
Long Life Unsweetened Red Grape Juice
Long Life Unsweetened Tomato Juice
Long Life Unsweetened White Grape Juice
Pure Orange Juice
Sparkling Apple Juice
Sparkling Red Grape Juice

*New to range.

SAINSBURYS
Foods with less than 5 per cent added sugar. (The products listed may be subject to change in ingredient or formulation and are intended as a guide only. 1984.)

Cereals
Bran Muesli
De Luxe Muesli
Hot Oat Cereal

Hot Oat Cereal and Bran
Mini Wheat
Puffed Wheat
Wholewheat Bisk
Wholewheat Mini Flakes

Desserts and Dessert Mixes
American Pancake Mix
Custard Powder
Pancake Mix

Fruit (canned)
Apple Slices
Apricots in Fruit Juice
Grapefruit Segments in Natural Juice
Orange Segments in Natural Juice
Peaches in Fruit Juice
Pears in Fruit Juice
Pineapple Slices in Natural Juice
Raspberries in Apple Juice
Strawberries in Apple Juice
Unsweetened Apricot Halves in Fruit Juice
Unsweetened Fruit Cocktail in Fruit Juice
Whole Mandarin Segments in Juice

Fruit Juices
Long Life Apple Juice
Long Life Orange Juice
Long Life Pure Jaffa Grapefruit Juice
Long Life Pure Jaffa Orange Juice
Natural Grapefruit Juice
Natural Orange Juice
Pure Concentrated Jaffa Orange Juice
Pure Pineapple Juice
Tomato Juice
Unsweetened Jaffa Grapefruit Juice
Unsweetened Jaffa Orange Juice

Spreads and Preserves
Crunchy Peanut Butter
Smooth Peanut Butter

TESCO

No Added Sugar

Cereals
Wholewheat Muesli Cereal

Drinks
Freshly Squeezed Orange Juice
Pure Apple Juice
Pure Grapefruit Juice
Pure Jaffa Orange Juice
Pure Orange Juice
Pure Pineapple Juice

Fruit (canned)
Fruit Cocktail in Natural Juice
Grapefruit Segments in Natural Juice
Pear Halves in Apple Juice
Pineapple Slices in Natural Juice

RECIPE LISTINGS

Biscuits/Cookies
Banana Finger Biscuits
Caraway Crackers
Carob Clusters
Chessey Straws
Coconut Biscuits
Date Flaps
Ginger Boys
Nut Drops
Peanut Butter Digestives

Breakfast Foods
Breakfast Muesli
Muesli
Warm Starter

Cakes/Buns/Teabreads
Bread Pudding
Christmas Cake
Curd Tartlets
Date Cake
Dark Apricot Gâteau
Dark Banana Buns
Dark Carob Slices
Eve's Drop Scones
Fig and Almond Bakewell
Fig Scones
Figgy Rolls
Golden Pineapple Teabread
Hot Cross Buns

Orange Raisin Cake
Rock Buns
Simnel Cake
Spiced Tea Bread
Truffles

Drinks
Apple and Carrot Juice
Apple and Orange Cup
Banana and Yogurt Drink
Fruit Cup
Nectar Shake
Strawberry Shake

Fruit Desserts
Apple Flake Pudding
Apple Fool
Apricot Crêpes
Apricot Steamed Pudding
Avocado and Coconut Creams
Avocado and Orange Cream
Blackcurrant and Apple Dessert
Citrus Trifle
Dutch Apple Tart
Exotic Fruit Salad
Fresh Fruit Salad
Fruit Compote
Fruit Crumble
Fruit in Jelly
Fruit Purée

Fruit Yogurt
Hawaii Rolls
Orange Cheesecake
Prune Blancmange
Strawberry Flan
Stewed Fruit
Tutti Fruiti
Upside Down Pudding

Ice Creams
Apple Ice Cream
Banana Ice Cream
Cashew Sorbet
Fruit Ice Cream
Knickerbocker Glories

Icings
Apricot Spread
Banana Nut Spread
Carob Spread

Milk/Yogurt/ Cream Cheese Desserts
Apple Flake Pudding
Baked Egg Custard
Chocolate Pots
Citrus Trifle
Fromage Blanc
Fruit Yogurts
Golden Rice Pudding
Orange Choc Pudding
Prune Blancmange
Queen of Puddings

Pastry Desserts
Cheese 'n' Apple Turnovers
Dutch Apple Tart
Festive Slices
Fig and Almond Bakewell
Figgy Rolls

Strawberry Flan

Salads
Exotic Fruit Salad
Fruit Salad
Spring Salad

Sauces
Baked Egg Custard
Custard Sauce
Mock Chocolate Sauce
Orange Foam Sauce
Tomato Sauce

Savouries
Avocado and Walnut Dip
Caraway Crackers
Cheese 'n' Apple Turnovers
Cheesy Straws
Chilled Soup
Fondue Sauce
Pinwheel Sandwiches
Pizza Quiches
Sandwich Fillers
Savoury Burgers
Savoury Caraway Slice
Spring Salad
Tomato Sauce

Snacks
Cheesey Straws
Popcorn
Rusks

Others
Almond Paste
Blackcurrant and Apple Butter
Chocolate Nests
Christmas Pudding
Crêpes
Fruity Marbles
Mincemeat
Nut Butter

BIBLIOGRAPHY

Bailey, Adrian and Dowell, Philip, *Book of Ingredients*, Michael Joseph, 1980.
Besford, John, *Good Mouthkeeping*, Oxford University Press, 1984.
BMA Board of Sciences Report on Diet, Nutrition and Health, 1986.
British Nutrition Foundation Report on Sugar, 1986.
Collier's Encyclopedia.
Cook, Richard and Elizabeth, *Sugar Off*, Great Ouse Press, 1983.
Horsley, Janet, *Sugar-Free Cookbook*, Prism Press, 1983.
Ministry of Agricultue, Fisheries and Food 'Consumption Levels Enquiry' Annual Report, 1984.
NACNE Report, 1983.
Sugar Consumption in Britain by A. J. Rugg-Gunn RH, BDS, PhD, FDS, 1986, BDJ.

INDEX